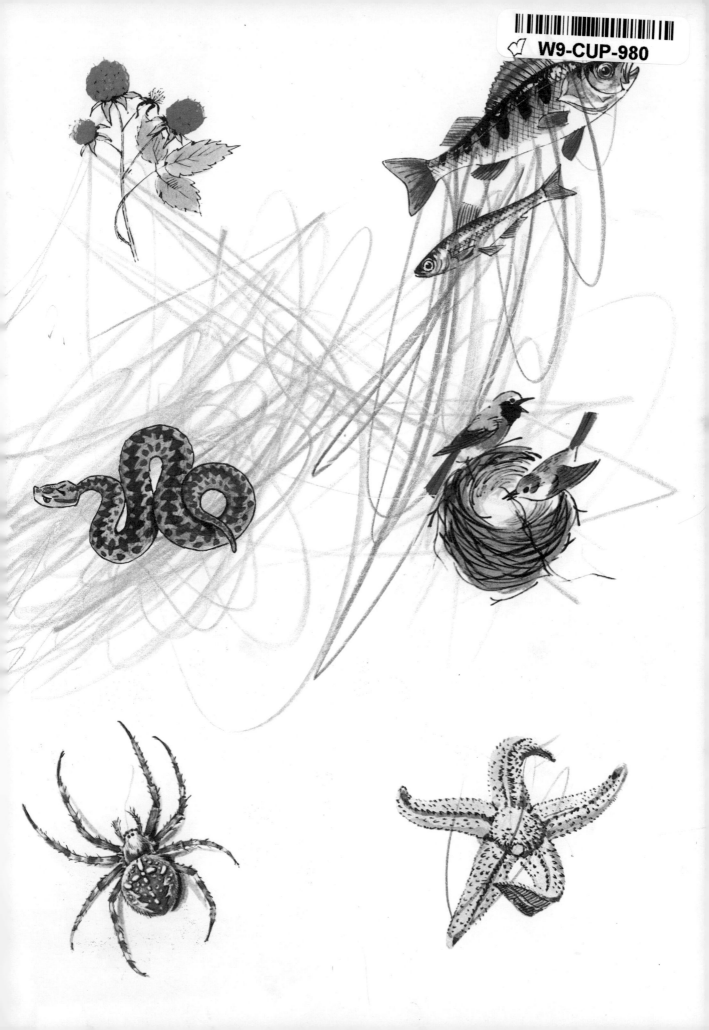

NATURE
Around the Year

By Henri Leclercq

Translated by Maureen Hornsey

Illustrated by Pierre Probst

GOLDEN PRESS • NEW YORK
Western Publishing Company, Inc.
Racine, Wisconsin

Foreword

Every month something different is happening in the world of nature, and all living things—animals, birds, fishes, plants, insects, and men—take part in this yearly cycle.

There are many exciting things to discover and to know about in the ever-changing world around us. Why do animals hibernate? What causes summer storms? What is photosynthesis? Why do birds migrate? How and when do tadpoles turn into frogs? What causes spring tides? How do plants grow, and why do the seasons change?

This beautifully illustrated book from France answers these and dozens of other intriguing questions as it describes and explores, month by month as season follows season, the extraordinary variety of nature and the changes which take place throughout the year in many different countries.

After reading about the natural world within these pages, we hope you will go on to make your own observations of what is happening around you. Then you will quickly discover that your own garden or park or countryside is full of life, too. Perhaps you will even find animals and plants that you have never noticed before as you watch and enjoy the changing seasons with fresh eyes.

Contents

WINTER

The Silent Forest

It is winter. Everything looks dark and drab in the silent, deserted forest. Any movement is muffled by the thick carpet of dead leaves. The sun stays low over the horizon, often hidden by mist all day long.

Everything seems to be dead. It is so cold that the streams are frozen over and all the cold-blooded creatures have fled to remote hiding places. They don't have to conserve their body heat as warm-blooded creatures do; their bodies are at the same temperature as their surroundings. They hide in logs, in heaps of stones and especially in the warm protective earth. The temperature would have to fall extremely low for the frost to penetrate the soil, with its blanket of dead leaves, to a depth of more than a few inches. Sheltered in the earth, motionless and sleeping, are the insects that were swarming about all summer: dung beetles, ground beetles, scarabs, stag beetles with their magnificent horns, glowworms, hawkmoths and many others. They would be difficult to recognize now; most of them are tightly enclosed in a protective case (a chrysalis), where they sleep peacefully. They are still alive, but they are living in slow motion and, during this time, mysterious changes are taking place inside the chrysalises.

Other creatures have taken shelter deep within the trees. The spider, for example, warmly wrapped in a silky cocoon, is safe under a loose piece of bark.

The earthworm is under the ground, where, like the mercury in a thermometer, it moves up or down according to changes in temperature. It may even emerge from the soil altogether in bright sunshine.

Vipers, adders and blindworms sleep 12 or 16 inches below the ground. The frogs have buried themselves in the waterlogged mud at the bottom of the pond; the toads are deep down in the earth, too deep to be affected by the cold.

They are all marking time, waiting for spring.

Even the trees are involved in this winter retreat. The sap which flowed freely through their branches in the summer almost ceases to flow in winter. Many trees lose their leaves and look almost dead. Despite this, there is still a lot of strength left in a tree. Even though its branches are bare, they don't snap like deadwood and it would take a lot of twisting and wrenching to tear one from its trunk.

While the cold-blooded animals lie dormant, the warm-blooded ones are fighting against the cold to maintain their body heat. But food is scarce at this time of year. They must conserve their energy, use their cunning, and sleep whenever possible.

Some animals solve the problem by taking cover. The European fallow deer, for example, camouflages himself with dead bracken. He lies motionless but still alert, ready to flee from an attacker.

The solution for the dormouse and the hedgehog is to hibernate. Other animals do not sleep all the time: squirrels can be seen occasionally in midwinter, when they wake up to have a nibble from their food store.

The forest is not an inviting place in the depths of winter. People, like animals, prefer to stay close to the warmth and comfort of their homes.

13

Life from the Sun

Life goes on at a slower rate in the winter because all living things are waiting for spring and the sun. All heat comes from the sun; without it, there would be no form of life on Earth.

The sun is not often visible in winter, but its heat is still present in the form of fire.

Early man made his fire of wood. Wood comes from trees, and trees absorb sunlight as they grow. You could say that the flames rising from a log fire are actually the summer sunlight stored in the wood coming back to life again in the winter fire.

A coal fire is another form of heat from the sun (solar heat), because coal itself was once wood. A long time ago, long before the days of primitive man, the earth was covered with huge forests. As the trees died, they fell to the ground and, layer on layer, they were pressed down to form the black stone known as coal.

Even electricity, a source of heat more widely used today, originates from the sun. It can be produced in a power station which is run on coal, and therefore run on sun-power; or it can be produced by turbines powered by water pressure. Even this water would not be available without the sun. Heat from the sun causes water to evaporate from the surface of the sea. This water vapor rises, clouds form and grow heavy, rain falls and fills the rivers. As they flow seaward, the rivers are harnessed to drive the turbines.

Fire has been a symbol of life and security ever since cavemen worshiped it as their only source of light and warmth and their main protection against wild animals. The fire is still the center of many homes.

Primitive man could produce a flame by rubbing sticks together, but the nature of the flame was a mystery to him. Scientists have since been able to explain something of the mystery.

Every object is made up of minute particles, called molecules, which cannot be seen by the naked eye. These molecules move all the time, but the movement is only slight when the object is cold.

When it is heated, the molecules begin to move about more vigorously and energy is released. This energy is spread to neighboring particles, causing warmth, or fire.

But even with plenty of fuel, this process would cease and the fire would die out if a particular gas which is present in the air were no longer available: this gas is oxygen. Oxygen itself cannot burn, but it is an essential part, or agent, of the burning process (combustion). We cannot see oxygen, but if it were not present, there would be neither fire nor life. As the flames begin to die down, you have only to blow on them, increasing the oxygen supply, and they will spring up again.

Winter is a time when all living things depend on reserve supplies, keeping themselves alive as best they can until the direct warmth of the sun returns with the coming of spring.

For millions and millions of years, the sun nourished huge forests. As the forest trees fell, they were buried beneath deep layers of soil and gradually turned into coal. Occasionally, prints of leaves from these forests of the Carboniferous Period are found on pieces of coal.

Imprint of a fern leaf on a piece of shale

Water

There is water everywhere you look. Perhaps it is not immediately apparent because it is not always a liquid; water can appear in many other forms.

There is more water on the earth's surface than anything else. There is water at the poles, but it is present in the form of ice because the rays of the sun don't give enough warmth to melt it. It is from the polar ice caps that pieces break away and float out to sea as icebergs. There is water at the equator, too; there it produces such dense vapor that it sometimes prevents the burning rays of the sun from scorching the earth.

In the human body, in plants and in animals, water takes up more space than any other single substance. If it suddenly vanished from the body, only a few handfuls of solid matter would be left.

Water seems easy to handle at first. It takes on the shape of any pot you pour it into and reliably flows down from higher to lower levels. But it is deceptive. When there are changes of temperature, it is not so predictable. As soon as the thermometer falls to 32°F, water freezes—it turns into ice. When water is heated to a temperature of 212°F, it boils; then it turns into an invisible gas called water vapor. Boiling is not the only way to turn water into vapor. As you have probably noticed, water left standing in an open pot in a warm room will slowly "disappear," or evaporate. Heat in the air changes the liquid into vapor. When

water vapor comes into contact with colder air, it condenses, becoming visible again as droplets of water.

Water has many other strange properties. It is at its heaviest at a temperature of 40°F and, as ice, it floats on water like a cork even though it is solid.

The water on the earth's surface is always on the move, according to the changes in the weather. It spurts up through the ground as a spring and then tumbles down toward the sea, first as a mountain stream and then as a broad river swollen by its tributaries. In this way the water from the spring becomes a part of the vast ocean and, as the sun beats down upon it, it will evaporate and form a cloud. This cloud of water vapor will then drift over the land. If the weather turns cooler, the vapor will condense into droplets of water which will grow larger and larger until they fall to the ground as rain. Back on the ground, the water filters down into the depths of the earth, and from there it will eventually leap up again as a spring. The whole cycle will then begin once more.

Water is affected not only by heat and cold but also by air pressure. The air that surrounds the earth exerts pressure on the water at the rate of 14.7 pounds per square inch. That means that, just over an area as small as a fingernail, the air is pressing down like a two-pound weight.

The air pressing down on the water prevents it turning into vapor and escaping. But if that air should become lighter, if its pressure should decrease, the water would quickly turn into vapor and rise, perhaps forming clouds in the sky. If, on the other hand, the pressure of the air were to increase, the water would remain in its liquid form. This is partly the reason why, when the barometer shows high atmospheric pressure, fine, clear weather is indicated.

Water can absorb many substances. A lump of sugar dissolves in it and seems to disappear. It hasn't really; it is all over the glass or jug which holds the water. But you can't take the sugar out again; it can only be recovered if the water evaporates completely. Salt too dissolves easily; seawater contains mountains of salt.

But the composition of water is the most astonishing thing of all. When people talk about water, they usually mean the liquid you drink or swim in. But when the scientist analyzes this familiar liquid, separating the different elements of which it is composed, his result is very surprising. He finds not a single drop of liquid, but two gases: oxygen and hydrogen.

Water is not as simple a substance as it seems at first.

Water has many forms. As a vapor, it is invisible. As it cools, it condenses into rain and eventually flows into rivers. Cold solidifies it and it becomes ice. As seawater evaporates, it rises into the sky, leaving behind the salt it contained.

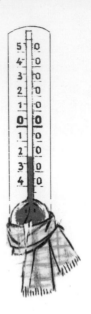

In the polar oceans, often covered with ice, boats become imprisoned in the ice cap. Nowadays special ships called icebreakers manage to break through.

JANUARY

Bitter Cold

In January the temperature often falls to freezing point (32°F at sea level) during the night. By morning, the roofs, the trees and the grass have all turned white, and well-known scenes look unfamiliar. Every drop of water or slightest trace of moisture has changed into specks of frost which sparkle in the bright winter sunshine.

During severe cold spells the thermometer may register 20°F, and if any place is unlucky enough to register zero or less, the event is likely to get special mention on television and in the newspapers. Old people talk about winters of long ago when the rivers were frozen over and you could cross them on foot, or when trees were struck dead by cold in the night and fell to the ground with a sinister groan.

Suitably protected, human beings can survive in temperatures much lower than those usually encountered in January. Pilots and astronauts fly up into the sky unworried by temperatures of –40°F or –60°F outside their craft. In Russia, at a place called Verkhoyansk, men live through midwinter at an average temperature of –58°F. The polar regions are always covered with ice, and sometimes boats and their crews are trapped there for long periods.

The lowest official temperature on the North American continent was recorded in the Yukon in 1947; it was –81°F. To produce even colder temperatures, man has to take over from nature. His technique is simple. It is based on the following principle: for a liquid to turn into gas, it must absorb heat from whatever material is nearest to it, thereby cooling that material. This principle can be tested just by dipping your hands in water and then allowing the water to evaporate; as the water changes from liquid to gas, it absorbs the heat it needs from your skin and your hands feel colder. Using this principle, man has invented refrigeration. To cool a refrigerator, he uses a circuit in which a liquefied gas changes back into dry gas and absorbs heat from the inside of the refrigerator in the process.

Different gases liquefy at different temperatures. Oxygen liquefies at –299°F, nitrogen at –346°F and a rare gas, helium, at a temperature as low as –452°F.

At these extremely low temperatures, strange things happen. If an eel is plunged into liquid nitrogen, it becomes as hard as rock; it could be broken to bits with a hammer. But if it is dropped into warm water again, it starts to wriggle; it is not dead. Once, in Siberia, a mammoth was found intact, preserved by the ice. The explorers' dogs were fed on mammoth that had been dead for thousands of years!

What happens when the temperature falls below the –452°F of liquid helium? The answer is bewildering: if the cold were to become still more severe, molecules would stop moving, and at temperatures below –459°F matter would cease to exist!

A gigantic mammoth with enormous tusks has been recovered intact, frozen stiff by the Siberian cold. It had been dead for thousands of years.

Winter Birds

It is so cold that the air feels taut. The least sound rings out across the countryside and vibrates in the vast silence. Even the wind seems to be frozen stiff.

When it is as cold as this, the birds who have not migrated for the winter may need help if they are to survive. They welcome seeds, bread crumbs and scraps sprinkled on the lawn and pieces of fat wedged in the bushes. They need drinking water, too, and since it quickly freezes over, it must be continually replaced.

The boldest birds, the sparrows, arrive as soon as the food is thrown out. They look more like little balls, with their feathers fluffed up to give them better protection from the cold. The one with the black bib is the male. The female

is gray and has a fat, cone-shaped beak; she is more timid. After the first sparrow, others appear as if from nowhere, perhaps summoned by the continuous twittering, and they squabble loudly over every scrap.

Sometimes the black-capped warbler appears among the sparrows. He is easily confused with the female sparrow, but he is slimmer, more elegant and has a more delicately shaped beak. He does not always go off with the other warblers to winter in warmer climates.

Blackbirds will often join in, too. The male, with his yellow beak and round beady eyes, is always alert to the slightest danger. The grayish-brown female, who is less sociable, will probably not stay, but will come back later. It will

be calmer then without the sparrows, who raise the alarm at every passing shadow or rustling leaf.

The chaffinch is also grateful for help. He is more colorful than the sparrows, though still not decked out in his full spring splendor. His head feathers have not yet turned to bronze, but he is easily recognized by his pink breast and his dark blue-and-white wings.

The tits ignore the seeds and the bread. They make for the fat and peck away at it, often upside down. Their undersides are yellow with a black band and their heads black with white cheeks.

The robin usually comes along, too. He is perhaps a favorite because he is sometimes the boldest of them all. He certainly justifies his second name: "red-breast." He looks so delicate, and his claws are as fine as wire; it is amazing that he can survive the cold. He hates

In winter, when the ground is covered with snow and there is no food, the birds pictured above depend on human aid. They are, from left to right, sparrows, starlings, the chaffinch, crows, the blackbird, the robin and tits.

crowds and noise, but if he notices anyone in the garden sawing a few logs or turning the soil over, he is there in a flash; he is so inquisitive that he can't resist coming up close to watch.

If the cold spell is prolonged, those birds that usually keep their distance in the fields and woods come closer to houses. Redwings and perhaps waxwings leave their lookout posts in the treetops and venture nearer.

Hunger drives the starlings nearer, too. Their dark, shaggy feathers stand out against the snow. They walk with ungainly, staccato steps like a brood of fat chickens. They are bold and arrogant and, if no one interrupts them, they quickly make off with every scrap of food that is available.

21

Why Trees Are Important

In the deserted forest the silence is broken by a rhythmical knocking: the sound of the wood-cutter's axe. It is soon followed by the rasp of a saw. Finally comes the long, creaking groan as the trunk of a tree is separated from its stump and crashes to the ground in a flurry of breaking branches.

In the clearing there are other trees that have been felled, waiting to be taken to the sawmill. Loads and loads of trunks and branches are waiting to be carted away. Thousands and thousands of things will be made from these trunks and branches—houses, furniture, paper, even toys. You can probably think of many other things we wouldn't have if there were no trees.

But all these trees that have been cut down should be replaced by new seedlings, because if there were no living trees or other green plants, we could not survive on Earth.

All our food comes first from green plants, directly or indirectly. Animals of all kinds, as well as people, eat vegetation and other food provided by plants. Even fish need green plants to live.

But plants do not need to eat other plants or animals for food; they can make their own food. The green parts of a plant do this by making food from carbon dioxide and water.

The process by which plants make this food is called photosynthesis, which means "building with light." Four things are necessary before photosynthesis can occur: green leaves, carbon dioxide (which is a gas that is found in the air), water, and sunlight. During the process of photosynthesis, the plant makes a form of sugar called glucose; this is its "food."

Glucose is made up of carbon, hydrogen and oxygen. The plant gets the carbon that it needs from the carbon dioxide in the air, which enters the plant through pores in its leaves. It gets the hydrogen and oxygen from water, which it absorbs from the soil.

Photosynthesis occurs only in the green parts of a plant. The green parts of plants contain chlorophyll, which gives the leaves their green

color, and which is necessary for photosynthesis to take place.

Here, water and carbon dioxide are combined chemically (broken down and re-built) by means of the chlorophyll to form glucose. In the process, extra oxygen is given off.

Sunlight is vital to the process because only light can provide the energy needed to make these changes.

In special cells of the plant, the glucose combines with minerals and other elements from the soil to make starches, fat, protein, and other foods which help the plant to grow in the same way that food helps us to grow. The plant also stores some of its food for later use in its roots, stems, seeds, and fruit—which we are then able to eat.

But this is not the only way green plants help us. Animals and human beings need oxygen to live. By taking in carbon dioxide and giving off oxygen, plants help "purify" the air by maintaining a proper balance between these two gases.

So trees and green plants are necessary for the food we eat and for the air we breathe. And if they decided to go on strike, we couldn't live on Earth.

FEBRUARY

Body Heat

The ice on the pond is good and solid, and people are skating. Everyone is laughing. Eyes are shining, cheeks are glowing.

It is amazing that everyone can be so hot when the weather is so cold, but there is a good reason for it: the human body produces heat, in the same way that a boiler does.

Any explanation of this process must start with the sun, for without it, there would be no form of heat on earth. The sun makes the vegetables grow, nourishes the grass for the cattle to graze on and ripens the grain to feed the poultry. The sun produces food, and food is the body's fuel; this is what the body uses.

The body's fuel is composed of substances containing carbon. This fuel is chewed and swallowed and then it passes into the bloodstream through the walls of the alimentary canal (the intestines).

Wood can only burn in the presence of oxygen from the air. The same is true of the substances which fuel the body and which are carried to the muscles by the bloodstream. Both "fires" work in the same way: as the supply of oxygen is increased, the fuel is used up more quickly and more energy is produced.

Oxygen from the air enters the body during breathing. Air reaches the lungs through the nose (and sometimes through the mouth). The lungs are like two sponges, and their walls are well supplied with blood, which is pumped into them in waves by the heart. When you hold your wrist to take your pulse, what you feel is the blood surging through the arteries in response to each heartbeat.

It is in the lungs, through very delicate membranes, that the blood absorbs the oxygen which it will carry to all parts of the body. This oxygen will allow the body, especially the muscles, to use the fuel which it has extracted from its food. Of course this process produces no flame, but, like burning, it does produce heat: it maintains a constant temperature of 98.6°F when the body is working normally.

Obviously, in a machine as complicated as the human body, the mechanism is not simple, but it can still be compared to a fire burning continuously.

When you have had a good meal, you are like a boiler that has just been stoked, and you feel very warm. But when you are hungry, you feel cold and have no energy. If you take part in some violent activity, like skating or football, you breathe faster and more deeply and so take in more air. The blood circulates more quickly from muscles to lungs and from lungs back to muscles again. The heart beats strongly. You feel uncomfortably hot: too much heat is being produced.

When skaters first go out on the pond, their feet feel frozen and their cheeks cold. Their caps are pulled well down over their ears and

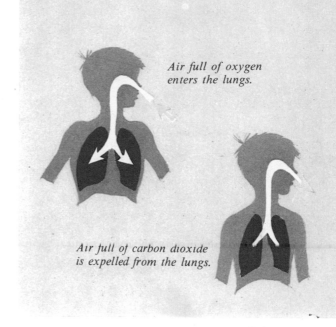

Air full of oxygen enters the lungs.

Air full of carbon dioxide is expelled from the lungs.

their scarves are wrapped tightly round their necks. But in no time their cheeks are burning hot. They push their caps back and throw off their scarves. They each have their inner "fire" to keep them warm and they are enjoying the fresh air that keeps it "burning."

Physical exercise speeds up the heartbeat and the circulation of the blood. More air, full of oxygen, enters the lungs. The body's inner "fire" burns more strongly and you feel warm even though the weather is very cold.

25

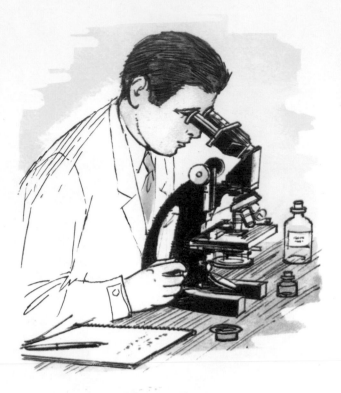

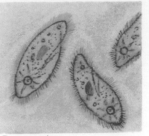
Paramecium

Stentor

FEBRUARY

The First Animals

February is the month of colds and flu. Each time an invalid recovers, it is a victory in the battle of life, but the victory is only won by destroying another life. The invalid recovers because one small kind of living matter, the white corpuscle in the blood, has killed another kind of living matter: the microbe or germ that caused the illness.

These battles, which are waged in the world of the infinitely small, involve life in its most primitive form.

Because microbes are primitive, that does not mean that their constitution is simple. Even the tiniest microbe is an example of life at an advanced stage of development: it is a universe of molecules and atoms.

An organism can only remain alive—that is it can only grow, feed, reproduce, react and defend itself—if it possesses a very sophisticated organization. Air, water, soil and even the human body are full of such organisms, so tiny that the human eye cannot even see the millions and millions of them swarming about.

One drop of water from a stream or pond examined under a microscope may show a whole world of minute creatures. Scientists have named them protozoa, which means first animals. They are first because they are in some ways the simplest; and also because perhaps they came first in the history of the world. It was hundreds of millions of years ago, in water, that the first protozoa, the very first animals, made their appearance. Since that time, animal life has become more and more complicated, but it has always progressed by means of the association and rearrangement of living elements, each like a single protozoan. These living elements are called cells. The human body contains about ten million billion (10,000,000,000,000,000) cells. Scientists who study them are called biologists.

These millions of cells in the human body have different jobs to do. You might almost compare the body to a very efficient town: some cells are responsible for food, some for defense, some for intelligence work, some for maintenance, and so on.

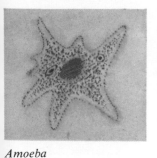
Amoeba

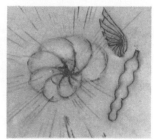
Foraminifer

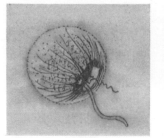
Flagellate

Radiolarian

The microscope reveals to the naturalist a world of infinite shapes and colors (above). When cells such as these unite, they form different types of animals which belong to the large family known as the invertebrates.

When the cells unite with one another, the living creature becomes larger and develops different organs. At this stage it can probably be seen by the naked eye.

Perhaps the simplest animals after the protozoa are those animals whose cells grow outward from a central point, like a ball or a star. The simplest are the sponges. Next in the scale are sea anemones and corals, which are fixed to the seabed like trees to the ground.

After these animals come those whose bodies are constructed around a central axis, along which run the alimentary canal and the nervous system. Included here are worms, mollusks (such as the snail or the mussel), crustaceans (such as crabs or lobsters), and spiders, centipedes and insects. Each of these different groups is one step further along the scale of development.

All these animals have one thing in common: they have no internal skeleton. They are called invertebrates, which means that they have no backbone. Such animals are found everywhere. They all have their different ways of living, different patterns of behavior and different instincts, and it is always fascinating to watch them whenever they appear.

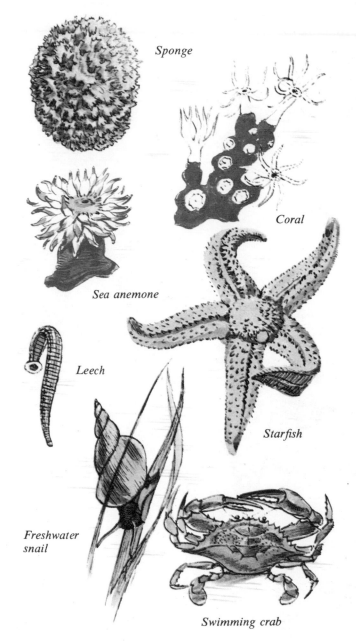
Sponge

Coral

Sea anemone

Leech

Starfish

Freshwater snail

Swimming crab

27

Spring Flowers

Patches of snow are still lying in shady corners and hollows; the sun, low in the sky, hasn't started to warm the frozen earth; but already there are signs that spring is coming.

According to the calendar, each season starts and finishes on a fixed date, but in fact the seasons develop and die away much more gradually. Spring has been developing quietly ever since the autumn and now the first signs are just visible.

It shows first on the hazel tree. As soon as all its leaves had fallen in November, preparations for spring began. By February its catkins, like grayish-colored caterpillars, are already out. A catkin is a pollen producer, and pollen is a special dust which every flower needs to produce fruit. The hazel tree is covered with thousands of catkins containing millions and millions of seeds whose only function is to help produce hazel nuts.

Finding these future hazel nuts is difficult because they are so tiny that they are almost invisible. They are little buds, close to the catkins. At the top of each bud is a crimson-colored tuft, splayed out so that it will catch the grains of pollen as they fall from the catkins. Both the tufts and the catkins are really flowers. The leaves of the hazel tree will appear

Well before the end of winter, the hazel tree is preparing itself for spring. Loaded with golden pollen, the catkins shine above the first buds (top). The buds are the future hazel nuts, ready to receive the pollen. Underground, frail shoots have pushed up from snowdrop bulbs (middle) and now they pierce the snow and come into flower (bottom).

later; at the moment they are still tightly rolled up inside their buds.

The forsythia also produces its flowers before its leaves. When it is in a sunny spot, an extravagant display of golden flowers appears on the bush. Their brilliant gold even shines through the snow which often settles on them as a reminder that winter is not over yet.

Another of the first spring flowers to appear, often when snow is still on the ground, is the snowdrop. Its delicate white flower hangs like a bell from the top of its stem. Since last summer the snowdrop bulb has been lying in the ground, holding the store of food which will eventually nourish a shoot and a flower.

The corms, or underground stem bases, of the crocus have been active all through the winter in the same way and now produce a fine display of purple, white and yellow crocus cups in the dark grass. When the flower blooms, the corm dies, but other corms lie beside those that are now in flower and they will produce flowers in following years. A crocus corm, like a tulip bulb, needs three years to mature and bear a flower.

There is still another flower belonging to the group that announces the coming of spring: the pansy.

The pansy is perhaps the most amazing of all, because not only does it appear early in the year, but it continues to bloom right through the winter. It fades in the December frost, but by January its shapely petals are unfolding again, like a highly colored butterfly.

The first flowers appear even while there are still traces of snow about. The crocuses bloom in the fields and, in the gardens, the forsythia is one big bouquet of yellow flowers, but without a single leaf.

FEBRUARY

The Fruitful Earth

The tractor drones across the field. The furrows appear in long straight lines behind it. The blades of the plough turn over the rich soil.

Many people think of soil as dirt, mud and dust. It is trampled underfoot without a thought, but this dark-colored layer, rarely more than a yard deep and lying above miles of rock and subsoil, is unique.

Man has worked out a lot of nature's mysteries, but he has not yet managed to make soil artificially. It would be an extremely difficult job. Just a list of its main ingredients—porous sand, non-porous clay and limestone—shows that it is a very complicated substance. It also contains tiny quantities of many important chemical and mineral substances such as nitrogen, phosphorus, iron, calcium, potassium, and magnesium.

Besides the mineral elements, soil contains all kinds of waste matter, animal and vegetable, which living organisms are continually discarding. All this matter, once decayed, combines with the mineral content to form humus, which gives that rich black type of soil all gardeners like. It is this organic matter that gives life to the soil.

Indeed, the soil is alive. Millions of little organisms (micro-organisms) assist the changes that take place within the soil, and these are so amazing that it is no exaggeration to call the soil an almost magical product.

A little hairy carrot seed, no bigger than a flea, can stay for years in its paper packet, completely dormant. But if it is dropped into the earth, a miracle occurs: a plant is born, takes root, pushes up its tiny shoot and opens its leaves to the air. The little seed has stored within it food that was produced by its parent

plant during photosynthesis, and, once it is planted in the earth, it will have all that it requires to produce a carrot, with its reddish coloring, its sweet flavor and its characteristic smell. In just the same incredible way, a grain of corn finds what it needs to produce a straw and a new ear of corn.

Of course, the conditions have to be right. The earth cannot create and nourish life without help. First it needs the sun to give heat and, with it, life. Next it needs water, to dissolve the mineral salts for the plants. Finally the earth needs air to provide oxygen, carbon dioxide and nitrogen.

It is fascinating to trace the soil through its changes into other materials. At first there is just dust or mud. A plant takes root in it and grows, using elements from the soil to nourish it. The soil has now, in a way, become food for man or animals. The human body is thus nourished by soil changed into other substances.

And every day the soil reclaims something from the living and the whole cycle begins again, producing other living things.

An Amazing Journey

Toward the end of winter, hundreds of tiny creatures that look like transparent worms appear in the streams of Europe. They are swimming purposefully upstream, but it is difficult to tell where they have come from or where they are going. These transparent worms are elvers, or baby eels.

In the middle of the Atlantic Ocean, hundreds of miles from land and where the water is warm, there is a special kind of sea. It is as big as several states put together and it is so thickly covered with sea plants (algae) that its surface looks like a grassy plain. You could almost walk on it. It is called the Sargasso Sea. Hidden beneath the algae there is a deep cavity in the seabed, hollowed out by the ocean.

In the bottom of this cavity the elvers are born. As soon as they hatch out, they leave the Sargasso Sea and head for streams and rivers in land areas where they will mature. Some swim westward to the rivers of the United States—a relatively short distance of a few hundred miles. But others set out on a long and amazing journey—to the inland streams

Three stages in the development of the elver

Facing page: *What a tremendous distance the eels cover on their trip to Europe! They set off from the Sargasso Sea (shown in green on the map) to come to rivers thousands of miles away, growing as they travel.*

of Europe, thousands of miles away. Here is the story of these elvers.

By the time they reach their destination in Europe, they have been traveling through the ocean non-stop for two years. They have come from the Atlantic, up the estuaries and rivers, and finally into the streams; they have never been there before but some unknown power guides them. When they first set out, two years before, there were millions and millions of them, all just a fraction of an inch long. Now they have grown a little bigger but their numbers have grown smaller, for their journey has been full of dangers. When they arrive, they immediately feel at home because they have come to the streams where their mothers once lived. All these elvers will be mothers too one day, for they are all females. The male elvers

Silver eel

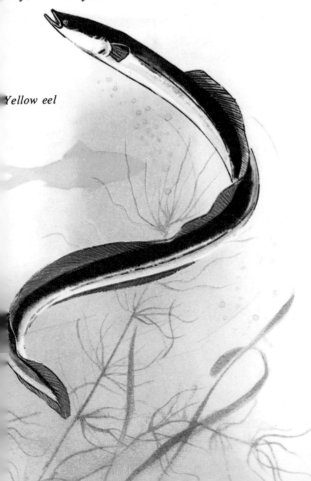

Yellow eel

do not come so far inland; they stay in the wide rivers and river mouths.

It takes twenty years for an elver to develop into a mature eel. The eel is a fish, not a snake. It breathes through gills, not lungs. The gills have such a small gill opening that the coat of moisture, which the gills must always retain if the fish is to be able to breathe, cannot evaporate. This means that, even though an eel is a fish, it can climb out of water at night and slide through the wet grass in search of other ponds and lakes.

When fully mature, the eels set out on their travels again. They will make the same journey they made as elvers, only in reverse this time. The female eels of Europe come from rivers in Germany, Holland, Belgium, Britain, France, Spain and other countries. They join the male eels in the Atlantic and continue their long journey deep in the ocean, returning to the Sargasso Sea where they were born.

MARCH

Training Trees

At the time when men were wandering naked and helpless through a hostile world, the dog must have been a type of wolf, self-willed and independent. A lot of time and patience must have been spent on making contact with him, and finally mastering and taming him. The well-trained dog of today can perform many difficult duties, like guarding a house, leading a blind man or tracking a criminal.

The cat and the horse were once wild too; both are tame now.

Animals are not the only things that can be trained or domesticated: trees can be as well. The fruits of wild trees—the sour cherry, the crab apple, the tiny, rock-hard pear—would be very unpleasant to eat. They are a far cry from the delicious apples, succulent pears and fat juicy cherries in the fruit store. These fruits are the results of a lot of hard work. Wild trees had to be trained to produce them. Scientists who study how to domesticate trees are called horticulturists.

One way of domesticating a wild tree is to provide it with some living material from a cultivated tree. It doesn't need much; just a twig with a few young buds is usually enough.

For instance, a horticulturist can start with a wild pear tree as a "stock" and can make it yield a good crop of succulent pears by a pro-

Today's delicious fruits are the results of man's long struggle to domesticate wild trees. An ordinary tree needs only a little pruning (top). Espaliers, trees trained to grow flat against a support, are often attached to latticework (left).

34

Grafting allows horticulturists to grow new varieties of fruit, using a wild tree as a stock (left). Pruning restricts the flow of the sap and helps produce fruit buds.

ess called grafting. First he cuts the top off its main stem. Then he makes a slit in it and puts into the slit a stem cut from a cultivated tree. This new stem will grow with the wild tree and live on its sap. When the sap flows and the new stem starts to grow, it will produce leaves, flowers and fruit like those of its parent tree, and not like those of the wild tree.

Many trees have to be retrained each year, otherwise they would quickly return to their wild state.

Yearly training is carried out by a process known as pruning. The gardener acts while the tree is dormant. But, as he will have to cut the tree, he waits until a time when the sap will rise sufficiently to heal the wounds.

Many fruit trees are pruned in March. To prune successfully, the horticulturist has to know something about the tree, or he will trim in the wrong places. One of the tree's secrets is the movement of its sap. As it rises behind the bark, it is making for the highest possible point. So if the tree is left to its own devices, it will grow taller and taller and taller, and will neglect the lower branches, which will soon become deadwood.

But the horticulturist's aim is to produce more fruit, not more branches. So the first job is to take the pruning knife and shears and lop off those branches which seem to be trying to reach the sky. The stronger they are, the shorter they should be cut, but the smaller branches and twigs should be preserved.

The flow of sap must be directed in such a way that the buds will become flowers and then fruit. This is where the skill of the horticulturist comes in. If he prunes the tree too severely, the surplus sap will rise and give new branches, not fruit. To avoid this, branches should not be cut off completely, but shortened so that they produce branches and fruit as well.

A branch is usually cut just above its third bud, or eye, like the one in the picture above. When the sap rises, an offshoot develops at the top of the branch to draw off the excess sap and, below it, there grow two buds which will produce sprigs of leaves in the first year and flowers in the second.

Pruning is not always a straightforward as that, of course. Every tree or branch has ways of its own. It is by studying their ways that the horticulturist knows how to treat them so as to produce the best possible crop of fruit.

35

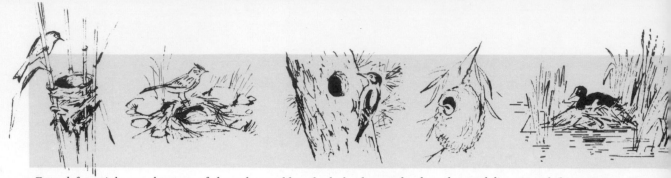

From left to right are the nests of the sedge warbler, the lark, the woodpecker, the penduline tit and the coot.

MARCH

Nests

During the winter many birds—blackbirds, chaffinches, sparrows, tits, robins, starlings— have come to depend on man for much of their food. But with the arrival of spring, they become independent again.

There are still very few insects about, so the ground is the most reliable source of food. The blackbird can often be seen on the lawn, pausing after each step and cocking his head to left and right. He seems to be listening to the ground, just as a doctor listens to his patient's chest. Perhaps he has heard a worm sliding along on its way up to the light. He stops and waits, motionless. All at once—flick!—his head dips down as if fixed to a spring that has suddenly uncoiled and he is pulling and tugging at a long worm with his beak.

The robin prefers to eat the little grubs that the gardener unearths as he digs the soil. The sparrow still hovers about close to the house, waiting for crumbs.

But for some time now another activity has become more important than the search for food. The change seemed to start on the day when the blackbird began to sing his dawn song again. That must have been the signal for the start of spring, for now the birds are busy all day hunting for building materials for their nests.

A gray female sparrow collects a piece of dry grass in her beak. She tries to pick up another piece and a twig as well, but the load is too heavy. She cannot fly properly with it, so she lands again. She puts her bundle down, picks it up piece by piece and flies up once again. This time she manages to reach the porch and there she starts to build her nest.

A female blackbird arrives, pulling behind her a piece of straw ten times her length. She slips in among the branches of the yew tree and the straw disappears after her. Meanwhile the female chaffinch is making her nest of bits of moss, lining the bottom with down.

Birds are very skillful builders: they weave together grass, straw, twigs, stolen scraps of wool, even hair. They work with their beaks, their wings, their feet, their tails, sometimes their whole bodies.

The finished nest is very strong. You often come across an old nest that has survived the winter wind and is still firmly fastened in the branches, sound enough to be used again in an emergency. However, few kinds of birds use the same nest two years running.

As soon as the nest is ready, the mother bird lays her eggs in it and then the long job of sit ting on them to keep them warm begins. The bird leaves them only rarely to feed.

There is a great fuss when the eggs hatch. The father is coming and going constantly, bringing tasty morsels back to the baby birds who are waiting with their mouths agape.

Of all the birds in the forest only one doesn't bother with construction work, and that is the cuckoo. The cuckoo raises her family at the expense of other birds: as soon as she comes across a finished nest, complete with eggs but with the parent birds temporarily away, she quickly lays her egg in among the others and leaves the job of caring for it to the other mother bird!

Chickens do not have to wait for their food like the nestlings. They can start pecking grain as soon as they emerge from their shells. They are so independent that the farmer doesn't need the hen, once she has laid the eggs. The chicks are often hatched in an incubator.

But the wild birds are more fascinating to watch than those in the farmyard. The parents work so hard all the time to rear their young, and watch over them so carefully when they attempt their hazardous first flight.

Once the young birds are reared and have learned to look after themselves, they leave the nest and eventually form new pairs. Their parents may then hatch out another clutch of eggs.

These chaffinches are busy preparing for their family. The hen bird is building the nest. She will lay the eggs in it and sit on them until they hatch. The cock bird will guard the nestlings and feed them.

More Home-Building

Even though the nights are still cold and frosty, the cats suddenly desert their favorite spot by the warm fire and stay out all night. They call across the rooftops to one another, shattering the stillness with their cries, and chase about madly. In the morning they return, wet and bedraggled, to the warmth and quiet of the house.

The dog, that model of devotion, does not usually leave his master's side for long, but he too may become fidgety and may go off on his own for a brief escapade.

Like the birds, animals grow restless as spring approaches for they are anxious to prepare for the birth of their young.

On the farm, the mother rabbit is busy with the fresh straw in her cage. She is scratching about in the darkest corner, piling the straw up and shaping it into a sort of nest by turning around and around in it. Soon she will be ready to line the nest, and she will use some of her softest fur, taken from the underside of her own belly.

The nest will be so carefully hidden under the straw that no one could spot it without disturbing the anxious mother.

In the woods, the female deer, or doe, has taken shelter in the thick undergrowth. She, too, has used her body to shape the branches into a little house which is sheltered by the surrounding trees. Thick ferns will serve to make it comfortable.

The cat needs a soft bed for her kittens too; a box lined with paper or rags and placed in a quiet corner is ideal. If a cat is disturbed when the kittens are new-born, or if danger threatens, then she will often move them to another, safer, place. This can be in a shed or even up a tree! The cat carries her kittens in her mouth. She picks one up by the loose fold of skin at the back of its neck and holds it like this, very gently, all the way to the new home. Then she returns and takes another, until finally all the kittens have been moved.

Most people feel very affectionate toward new-born animals and enjoy nursing and stroking a kitten or puppy. But the same people sometimes do not find a young toad or fish or bird in the least attractive.

There is a simple reason for this: human beings feel this attraction for the young of mammals because they are mammals themselves. Furthermore, all mammals are helpless at birth and depend on their parents for affection and food. They all have to be brought up—that is, taught to cope with life in an adult way—and they all learn to make noises to assist in communication with one another. In addition, human mammals have very much the same skeleton and organs as their animal counterparts.

Many mammals make nests of a kind for their young. In the woods, the doe makes a bed of leaves and branches for her fawn (facing page). Nearer home, the cat will find a cosy corner like this one up in the hayloft—unless someone has given her a basket lined with soft rags.

A bud is a kind of nest for the seed which will eventually develop into the flower and then the fruit of the tree. The future flower is well protected by these layers of scales and their lining.

MARCH

Buds

In spring everything in nature seems to be busy with the same task: producing and rearing young. Plants are busy too. They are producing the buds which contain the seeds of future plants.

Most buds are very small, but the horse chestnut is an exception. It produces a bud large enough to show that the preparations made for the new generation in the plant world are every bit as elaborate as those in the animal world.

Let us look at the bud at the tip of a branch (the terminal bud) and the future flower and fruit it contains. The outside of the bud is coated with a kind of resin which is very thick and sticky. Like a varnish, it protects the bud from damage by water, and it also traps insects before they can penetrate to the heart of the

bud. Under the coat of sticky resin lies a layer of scales which overlap like tiles on a roof, providing further protection against rain and insects.

Under the sticky scales are some soft green ones and then a fur-like lining. These two soft layers cushion the minute flower against severe cold and protect it from the constant battering of the wind.

They serve the same purpose as the down which lines the bird's nest or the soft fur that the rabbit spreads over the straw.

Safe in the heart of the bud is a little bunch of flowers folded round a tiny stem. When the flowers are strong enough, they will push out of the buds and, by May or June, the horse chestnut tree will be covered in white, or sometimes pink, flowers. By the time autumn comes the

flowers have fallen and, in their place, the fruit of the tree, the chestnuts, have developed.

The seed from which future horse chestnut trees will grow is the brown shiny "conker," which has been used for centuries in a popular children's game. This seed is at first protected in a round, green, spiky case. When the fruit falls to the ground, this outer case splits open and inside is the hard, brown, shiny "conker."

If you come across a chestnut that has been lying on the ground since the previous autumn, you may think it is dead, but if you bend down and look at it more closely, you will notice that its hard brown skin has split open and a strong root has grown from inside the chestnut to anchor itself in the ground. Growing upward from the same crack is a shoot bearing two tiny leaves. It was to make sure that young trees like this would grow that the trees and plants produced such carefully designed buds in the spring.

By autumn the horse chestnut flower has developed into the hard, shining brown chestnut. It is protected by a prickly outer case which splits open when the chestnut has fallen to the ground. If the chestnut stays undisturbed on the ground, a new horse chestnut tree will grow from it.

The Planet Earth

Millions and millions of years ago, a ball of fire appeared in space, perhaps having fallen away from the sun; it started to revolve around the sun as a satellite. This ball of fire became the Earth, and it is very small compared to the sun. It is like comparing the head of a pin to a football. The sun appears small to people on the Earth only because it is 93 million miles away.

If the Earth were simply revolving around the sun (rather like a wasp circling round a honey pot), the effect of this revolution on the

Figure 1 shows how the Earth would be illuminated by the sun if it were not tilted and did not rotate.
Figure 2 shows how the Earth would be illuminated by the sun if it were tilted but still did not rotate. It would always be dark at the North Pole, always light at the South Pole, and the hottest point would be somewhere on the Tropic of Capricorn.

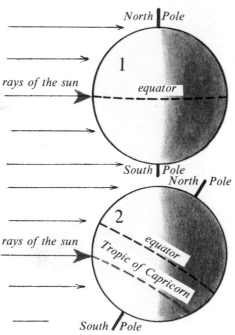

Earth would be easy to describe. One half of the globe would always be light and the other half always dark (below left, fig. 1). The hottest point on the globe would be on the equator which would always be nearest to the sun. In contrast, the poles, receiving no more than a glimmer of the sun's light over the horizon, would have permanent winter. In the United States and Europe, which are about midway between the equator and the North Pole, it would always be as warm as it is in spring. Every place on the Earth would have a constant temperature throughout the year.

But the movement of the Earth is much more complicated, and this explains why there are days and nights and changing seasons.

At the same time as the Earth is revolving round the sun, it is also spinning on its own axis, and it rotates 365 times before it returns to the same point again on its course around the sun. During this time, one year has elapsed. Because it rotates once in the course of each day, different parts of the globe are illuminated at different times, and so there are daylight and darkness.

The Earth rotates, but it does not rotate upright on its axis. The axis is tilted, or inclined, and this causes the change of seasons. It means that the equator is not always the point nearest to the sun, for sometimes the Tropic of Cancer or the Tropic of Capricorn is nearer and therefore hotter (left, fig. 2). It also means that at certain times of the year the North Pole

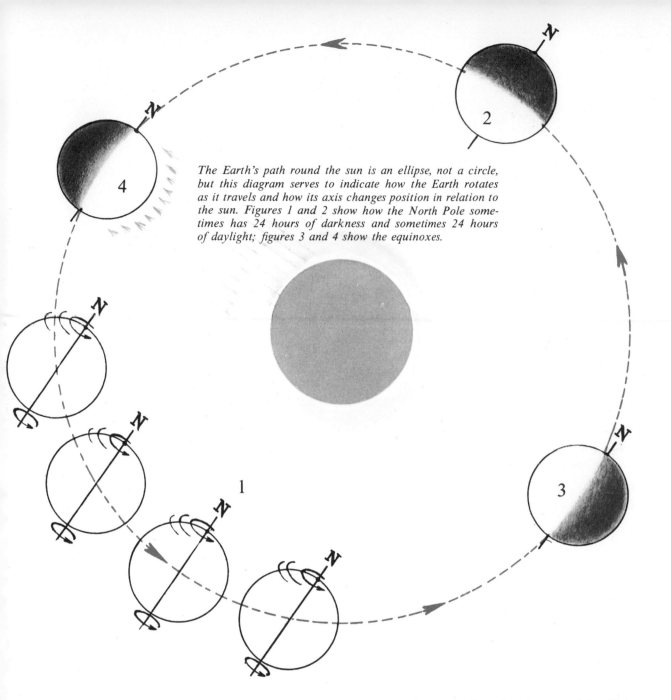

The Earth's path round the sun is an ellipse, not a circle, but this diagram serves to indicate how the Earth rotates as it travels and how its axis changes position in relation to the sun. Figures 1 and 2 show how the North Pole sometimes has 24 hours of darkness and sometimes 24 hours of daylight; figures 3 and 4 show the equinoxes.

s dark all day while the sun never sets at the South Pole; at other times, the situation is reversed (above).

Changes in the seasons are marked by the spring equinox and the autumn equinox, the two occasions in the year when the Earth's axis is in line with the sun. "Equinox" (a word derived from the Latin *aequus* for equal and *nox* for night) means that on these two dates of the year the whole of the globe has exactly twelve

hours of darkness and twelve hours of daylight. The spring equinox, on March 21st, marks the end of the darkest and coldest period for the North Pole and the beginning of spring in the Northern Hemisphere. The days have been growing gradually longer ever since the beginning of the year, but now the northern half of the globe will tilt gradually nearer to the sun and will begin to benefit from the greater heat and extra daylight of summer.

Ants

When ants are discovered in the house, there are indignant complaints and the ant powder is immediately brought out. Yet the ants have every right to be there; they first occupied the Earth millions of years ago, before the coming of the dinosaur, the mammoth or the bison. They will probably outlive man in the end.

The ant powder is effective, and dozens of dead ants have to be cleared away, but ants are not easily put off. If the house is temporarily closed to them, they will settle instead in the garden or the woods.

In their chosen spot, they construct their nest in the shape of a hill. They cover the top of the hill with twigs and dead leaves arranged in such a way that the rain will flow away from it. The hill is the top of a vast underground multi-story building, with thirty or forty floors and gently sloping access ramps.

Main and subsidiary roads lead away from the nest in all directions and teams of workers move along them all day long. Processions of "porters" carry home shoots, crumbs or dead insects for food. They pull and drag at their burdens, undaunted by any obstacle. They are very strong: an ant can move a weight twenty-five times that of its own body, which means that, relatively, it is twenty times stronger than a horse. If the ant cannot manage its load, it uses its antennae to call for help and every ant nearby joins in.

Some ants are "farmers." They tend herds of aphids which they keep in the bushes, rather as farmers keep cows. The aphids feed on the sugary sap of the plants they live on and collect a large amount of sugar in their bodies. The ants "milk" them of this sweet liquid by stroking them with their antennae.

Ants sometimes even appear to have their own gardens beside the hill, where they cultivate young shoots and patches of toadstools for use as food.

Anyone watching ants at work outside the nest would think that ant colonies are chiefly concerned with gathering vast amounts of food. But in fact there are many more ants busy inside the nest than outside, and they all have to be fed. There are the masons and the architects who erect and maintain the building; the nurse-maids who carry the eggs up to the top floor every morning to be warmed by the sun and bring them back to the basement in the evening to protect them from the damp; the nurses

Just as farmers rear animals to provide food, some industrious ants keep herds of aphids which feed on sap and are "milked" by the ants.

who look after the larvae and feed them with predigested juices from their own stomachs; the queens who lay the eggs. The eggs are minute, but they rapidly grow into larvae and then pupae enveloped in silky cocoons. They emerge from the cocoons as ants and immediately become workers themselves.

Sometimes ants of a different species from those occupying the nest are seen approaching it. They are prisoners of war, and they are surrounded by vigilant "soldiers." They will be put to work in the nest, rather like slaves.

The intelligence of ants is amazing. The large size of the head in relation to the body is a sign that their brain is much more developed than that of most insects.

People often destroy ants without a second thought, yet they perform a very valuable service by removing the decaying remains of dead animals.

Ants live in well-organized "cities." Some collect and store food (here they are seen bringing in a beetle), while others look after the larvae and pupae. The big ant in the center is the queen; she is laying eggs.

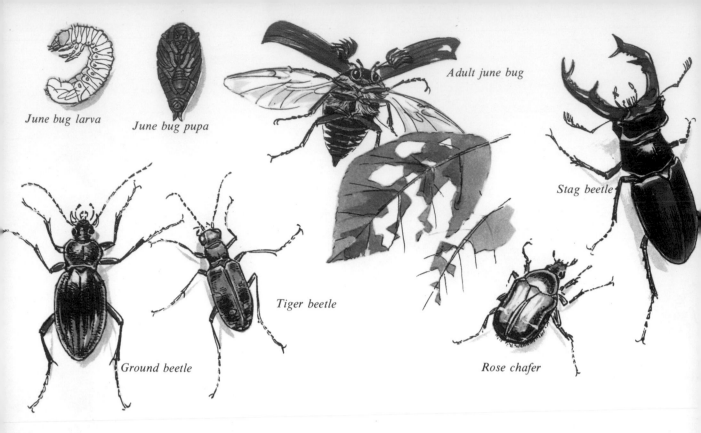

June bug larva

June bug pupa

Adult june bug

Stag beetle

Tiger beetle

Ground beetle

Rose chafer

MARCH

Masters of the Earth

We cannot ignore the "cousins" of the ants —all those animals belonging in the same classification and which, as much by antiquity as by number, are incontestably the masters of our earth: the insects.

There are insects everywhere except in the sea—in the house, in freshwater, in the air, on flowers and fruit, on animals, underground— and they all have their own ways of defending themselves, finding their food and caring for their young. They sometimes change their shape completely at different periods in their development (metamorphosis). At one stage they crawl, at the next they may fly. A fat, ugly caterpillar becomes a vivid and beautiful butterfly. Sometimes they are very active, but for a

long period they may remain dormant in a silky cocoon or a horny case (the chrysalis). It is difficult to believe that a motionless brown pupa started life as a greedy white grub and will soon continue as a clumsy june bug. This metamorphosis is complete only after three years.

There are some insects as big as a man's hand and some so small that they can only be examined under a microscope. There are over a million different species of insects, far more than the species of all other living creatures put together.

The body of an insect has three distinct parts: the head, the thorax (central portion) and the abdomen.

The head is equipped with feelers, or antennae, which often have a particularly acute sense of smell. Also on the head are the compound eyes, composed of many little facets and positioned in such a way that the insect can usually see behind and to the side. The mouth

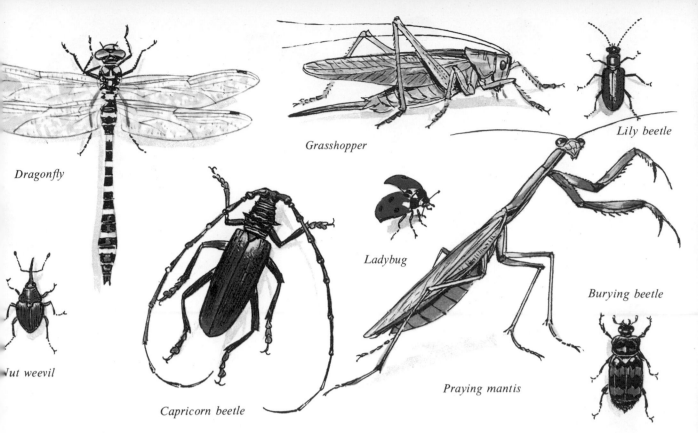

Dragonfly

Grasshopper

Lily beetle

Nut weevil

Capricorn beetle

Ladybug

Praying mantis

Burying beetle

varies with the different types of insects: the ground beetle has strong jaws (mandibles) for chewing and the butterfly has a proboscis, a sort of trunk which it unfurls to suck up nectar. The mandibles of one large beetle are huge in relation to the size of its body and look like antlers; as a result, it is called the stag beetle.

Attached to the central portion of the body, the thorax, are three pairs of legs and usually two pairs of wings. The wings of the butterfly are so bright and delicate that it looks like a moving flower. In most beetles, the fore wings are hard sheaths which fold over the thin membrane of the hind wings, the true flying wings, to protect them. The best known of these hard protective wings are probably the red ones with black spots belonging to the ladybug. Those of the ground beetle are hard and shiny like metal; those of the tiger beetle are an attractive green splashed with yellow.

The third part of the insect's body, the abdomen, is composed of segments. In some insects the abdomen is so flexible that it can roll right up, and an unwary person can be unpleasantly surprised by the sting that suddenly flicks out from it. Keep a wary eye, too, on the wasp and the hornet, whose stings can be painful and sometimes dangerous.

Though some insects are harmful and some are counted as pests because they attack vital crops, many are helpful, especially to the gardener: the ground beetle devours caterpillars and ladybugs feed on aphids.

Insects breathe, and they have a heart which pumps their colorless blood around their bodies. They also have a stomach, but, as they have no internal skeleton or backbone, they are classed as invertebrates.

Insects are striking examples of the working of instinct. The parents produce them as larvae, which eventually become pupae; by the time the pupae become mature insects, the parents are far away. The new insects must know by instinct all they need to know to survive.

SPRING

APRIL

Time to Get Up

Throughout the long, cold winter the dormouse, like the hamster and some other small mammals, has been in a special deep sleep called hibernation. Every autumn he gets ready to sleep through the winter in this way. He makes a safe nest, lined with moss, under the ground and collects food which he stores near the nest. He also eats a great deal while there is still plenty of food available. Then, as soon as the weather becomes colder, the days grow shorter, and food becomes harder to find, the dormouse settles down in his warm nest in the ground where he is safe from the frosts and snows to come.

During the deep sleep of hibernation the dormouse's heartbeats and his breathing become slower and his body temperature changes with the temperature of the air around him, just like a cold-blooded animal. It is this change in body temperature which is the important difference between hibernation and an ordinary sleep.

While the dormouse is asleep his body uses up the stored fat of his eating in the autumn. From time to time he wakes up and goes to his food store to eat, but he goes back into hibernation until the spring comes, snug in his bed of moss.

With the coming of warm weather the brown furry dormouse shivers suddenly, opens one eye and heaves a deep sigh. Several times already in recent weeks, when the warm rays of the sun have touched the bank above his hole, he has stirred and blinked and gone back to sleep again. But now it really is time for the young dormouse to shake himself and wake up after his first hibernation.

He breathes deeply. Gradually his heart begins to beat more strongly and warmth slowly spreads through his thin, cold body. For five months his body functions have been practically at a standstill, so it takes him some time to recover.

He stands up and yawns. Then he makes his way shakily out of his dark hole toward the light.

His is hungry. The garden, which was bare and empty when he left it last autumn, looks tempting now with its new green growth. But it is spring, and for the dormouse, as for all the other animals, the need to find a mate is more important than his need for food.

His long winter sleep has not made him less alert. As he sets off for the woods in the eve-ning, he is quick to crouch out of sight when he hears a rustle in the grass. The sound comes from a pair of hedgehogs out on their first nocturnal hunt since their winter sleep, searching for mice or snails or insects.

Another danger makes the dormouse take cover. This time it is the badger, who is also out hunting on this warm April evening. He has slept only during the coldest spells of the winter and in his wakeful periods he has continued to hunt for small mammals, birds, snails, frogs or toads. The badger is as big as a dog so he is like a monster to the dormouse. But the badger passes him by, and he is safe to continue his search for a mate.

By the pond the frogs have appeared once more. During the winter they burrow into the bottom mud of the pond to escape the cold. But now it is spring, and all the animals are active and searching for mates.

Toad

Green frog

APRIL

Amphibians: Creatures of Land and Water

Like all creatures in the spring, the toad, too, is getting ready to produce its young; it is on its way back to the pond where it was born.

The life story of a toad is fascinating, although the toad is very ugly to look at. It has short, fat legs and its skin is covered with warts. These warts contain a fluid that oozes out when the toad is threatened and helps to protect him from his enemies by making the attacking animal sick. This fluid is not poisonous to people and does not cause warts—although it can be very irritating if it comes in contact with the eyes or the mouth, or open cuts.

It is important not to harm the toad, because the gardener considers it his best friend. It can destroy insects at an amazing speed by flicking out its sticky tongue and trapping them on its surface.

The toad is especially interesting because, along with the frog, it is a member of the first group of vertebrates to leave the water and to survive on land. Such animals are called batrachians, or amphibians. But even today they still retain some of their former habits: they start life in the water, almost as fish, and live on land only when they are mature. It is because the young toads and frogs must hatch in water that the adults return to their ponds in April.

Female toads and frogs lay eggs, thousands and thousands of them. The common frog lays more than 4,000 eggs and the green frog more than 5,000. The eggs are only a tiny fraction of an inch long when they are laid but they are nevertheless very complex. They have the advantage, for the curious observer, of not being hidden by a shell like birds' eggs. Their development can be followed with the help of a magnifying glass at first, and later, as they grow bigger, with the naked eye.

After four or five days, the tiny toad or frog appears. It is a very crude creature. It has no limbs, just a tail, but even that is not powerful enough to make the creature mobile. It has two bulges for breathing, no eyes, no nostrils, and a sucker instead of a mouth.

It is exciting to watch how quickly the bulges become gills, which make it possible for the creature to use the oxygen from the water. Eyes and mouth form. The tail grows longer and becomes flexible. The animal is now a tadpole; it looks like a large head with a tail tacked on.

The development continues. At first it looks as if the tadpole is going to develop into a fish. It still breathes like a fish, taking water in through the mouth and absorbing oxygen from it as it passes out over the gills. But when the tadpole is twenty days old, back legs begin to appear and then front ones.

Now it seems to be neither tadpole nor frog. It still breathes like a fish but it moves like a frog. The tail shrinks and the legs start to fulfill their proper function.

After twelve weeks the gills also are lost and the lungs have to start taking in oxygen from the air. The young amphibian is leading a double life: it feeds underwater but it must breathe out of the water. Finally it leaves the pond altogether to start its life on land. It is still small, about half an inch long. A toad takes five years to reach its full size.

The mature toad or frog will live for 30, 40 or even 50 years and will return to the pond each spring, so that new offspring can be hatched that will live as their parents did—first in water and later on land.

The picture on the right shows the complete life history of the frog, starting at the bottom with the jelly-like spawn containing the egg. (In toad spawn, the eggs are contained in long strands of jelly.) The long-tailed tadpole emerges from the egg. Gradually the legs grow and the tail disappears. At the top is the adult frog; gills have been replaced by lungs and it is free to leap off into the fields.

APRIL

Weather

Weather is never very predictable, but in April it changes dramatically from minute to minute. Bright sunshine is suddenly blotted out by driving rain and sleet; and then, just a few minutes later, the wind has blown the rain clouds away and the sun is shining again from a clear blue sky.

Since Christmas, the sun has been rising a little farther to the left each day, climbing higher in the sky and setting a little farther to the right.

On the day of the spring equinox, it rose exactly in the east and set exactly in the west. It is because the position of the Earth in rela-

tion to the sun changes in this way that there are changing seasons.

Whatever the season, the weather on any particular day can be affected suddenly by the wind.

Wind occurs wherever there is warm air and cold air, and since on the Earth there are two poles which are cold and an equator which is hot, wind is inevitable. Warm air is lighter than cold air, so it rises and leaves room for heavier cold air to come in at ground level to replace it. This movement of air is wind. Coastal regions are often windy because the land warms up more quickly than the sea, so cold air from the sea is always moving in to replace the warm air rising above the land. Often, clouds of water vapor that have collected over the sea are blown in with the cold air.

It is easy to imagine the effects of a cold wind blowing from the North Pole. If it passes over clouds as it blows, it cools the water vapor in the clouds and rain falls. If it is so cold that it freezes the cloud, snow falls instead. If the icy wind blows when the rain is already falling, the rain gradually turns to hail.

The absence of wind can be a problem, too. If a cloud rests at ground level, there can be fog.

At all times of the year, the ground cools during the night. When water vapor, which has been present in the air throughout the day, comes into contact with the cold ground, it condenses into drops of water. This is the morning dew.

If the temperature falls very low, the water vapor in the air turns to particles of ice which are deposited on every leaf and stone. This is the frost that changes the most ordinary landscape into a spectacular scene.

In winter when the ground is frozen so hard that footsteps echo, the arrival of a warm wind bringing in air laden with water vapor can be very hazardous. As the water vapor comes into contact with the frozen ground, it freezes itself and becomes a layer of solid ice.

Since the weather is influenced by so many different things, it is hardly surprising that it should be so unreliable in April: the cold of winter has not quite disappeared and yet summer warmth is already having some effect. But April showers are not too hard to bear when they are just the necessary changes which show that summer is coming.

When water vapor, which is invisible in warm air, comes into contact with cold air, it condenses and may fall as rain.

Fog is a cloud at ground level.

Dew is water vapor which condenses into drops of water as it comes into contact with the cold ground.

In winter, the dew becomes frost.

Blossomtime

The showers have become less frequent. At last the sun is shining and buds burst open in the warm air. The fruit trees produce their flowers before the leaves; plum, cherry, peach and pear trees are one big mass of blossom. Every single bud on the cherry tree opens into a bunch of three or four flowers.

Each flower is attached to the cherry tree by its own stem, which is called the peduncle, the "little foot."

Attached to the peduncle, but now largely hidden by the open flower, are five green sepals, which originally protected the folded petals.

Each flower has five white petals. If the petals are pulled back to show the heart of the flower more clearly, some little yellow tufts fall out.

The flower of the cherry tree. The picture on the left shows the arrangement of the green sepals and the white petals at the end of the peduncle. The tip of the pistil surrounded by the yellow pollen-bearing stamens is just visible in the center of the flower. The section of the flower on the right shows the arrangement of the pistil and the stamens more clearly. Once the pollen has been deposited on the stigma at the top of the pistil, the flower fades and part of the pistil swells to form the cherry.

These look rather like straight pins with little heads, and there are about twenty of them in one flower. They are the stamens, and the heads of these "pins" contain pollen.

Pollen is essential if the flower is to produce a fruit, in this case a cherry. If the pollen grains were removed, the tree would be sterile.

When the sepals (collectively called the calyx) and the petals (called the corolla) are stripped off, it is possible to examine the tip of the peduncle. It is swollen into a little green ball, and rising up out of it is a narrow tube with a flattened top. The whole of this structure is called the pistil, and it is well concealed within the flower. Its ball-shaped base is the ovary and inside it is the seed of a future cherry tree. The tube to the ovary is called the style and the flattened top is called the stigma. The pollen will rest on the stigma when the flower is ready to be fertilized.

Once the pollen has been deposited on the stigma, the development of the cherry can proceed. Petals, stamens and sepals fall. A hard

wall encloses the developing seed and, around it, the ovary swells into a thick fleshy coat; this is the cherry. Its purpose is to protect the seed and to encourage animals to distribute it.

Most flowers are like those of the cherry tree: they have calyx, corolla, stamens and pis-til, but the shape, number and arrangement of these parts can be different. Plants whose parts have the same characteristics are grouped into "families." Scientists who study plants and their groups are called botanists; their work is very interesting and very important.

Bees

The fruit trees are covered with flowers and there are even more flowers in the fields and woods. It is an enormous task to make sure that a grain of pollen is deposited on the stigma of every single flower, so that its seed can be fertilized and a fruit can form.

Fortunately, in some flowers the stamens are so close to the stigma that fertilization takes place automatically, but, in addition, there are thousands and thousands of insects which carry pollen from flower to flower, sometimes over long distances.

There is a continuous humming and buzzing around a cherry tree when it is in blossom, and there are insects crawling everywhere: flies, wasps, ladybugs, ants and the busiest of them all, bees.

Insects are attracted to flowers by a sweet liquid which is secreted by the pistil. This liquid is so delicious that it is called nectar, the name given to the favorite drink of the Greek gods. The sweet, tasty pollen is also sought after by the insects. There is plenty of pollen to spare for the visiting insect: just one grain from all the thousands of grains of pollen which the flower produces is all that is needed to fertilize the seed. As the insect crawls into the flower to gather the pollen, on the way it accidentally deposits some grains on the conveniently placed stigma.

Honeybees play an important part in fertilizing the flowers and promoting the development of the fruit, but they don't do all this work for the sake of the flowers; it is part of the work they do for the benefit of the hive. The nectar and pollen they collect is taken back to the hive for general use.

The youngest worker-bees are on trial flights and they are the ones that collect pollen. The bees' hind legs are specially designed for the job. One segment of each hind leg is adapted to form a pollen basket and the segment below it is covered with rows of hairs or bristles like a brush. The bee uses these brushes to gather pollen and then, by crossing the hind legs and scraping them one against the other, it transfers the pollen into the basket that it has on the opposite leg.

To make sure that the pollen will not be lost during the return to the hive, the bee carries a few drops of honey which it uses as a kind of glue.

The more experienced bees collect the nectar, and it is estimated that one bee makes 20,000 flights to collect two pounds. The bee does not swallow the nectar because then it would be digested. Instead, it sucks the liquid into its crop, where chemicals start to convert it into honey. On returning to the hive, the bee regurgitates the contents of the crop, and the conversion to honey is finally completed in the hive.

When a bee has found some flowers that are particularly rich in nectar, it can "tell" the other bees where the flowers are. The bee does this by performing a special dance when it returns to the hive. The other bees gather around to watch. From the way the bee dances, they can tell how far away the flowers are, and in which direction.

The hind leg of the bee, showing the pollen basket empty on the left and filled with pollen on the right.

Bees at work on lavender flowers. The younger ones gather pollen. The older ones suck up nectar which will be made into honey.

59

The Potato Plant

Potatoes are believed to have originated in the Western Hemisphere. Spaniards invading South America brought back the first potatoes to Europe in the 16th century. Soon afterward Sir Walter Raleigh brought the first potatoes to England from North America. They didn't arouse much interest in Europe at first, but now they are eaten in large quantities in many parts of the world.

Even though the pretty blue flower of the potato plant gives us no hint of its underground secret, somehow people discovered that the yellowish swellings that form on the plant are nourishing to eat. Since its humble beginnings, the potato has been greatly improved by horticulturists. Next to rice, it is now the most widely eaten food in the world.

The potato plant reproduces by means of the potato itself (the tuber), and it is in April that the tuber becomes active. The true seeds of the potato yield very puny new plants. Small shoots, green and purple in color and protected by a coat of fine down, emerge from the top of the tuber—the side where there are most little scars, or eyes. These shoots bear buds which will grow into proper stems with leaves. Little white roots also emerge from the eyes.

Sometimes there is a thread, like a piece of old string, attached to the bottom of the potato; this is a remnant of the stem from which it developed the year before. A potato is not a root. It is a swollen stem, an underground stem which grows from the same main stalk which bears stems and leaves above ground.

The first shoots break through the soil a few weeks after the potato tuber is planted. As in all plants, the stems bear leaves and flowers and the flowers eventually form fruits; the fruits of the potato plant are like little green berries. Meanwhile, underground, other stems

The potato germinates in spring.

Once the tuber is planted, the shoots develop into stems.

develop and swell into potatoes. One potato tuber produces a lot of growth both above and below the ground, but since the gardener wants most of the stems to develop underground and swell into potatoes, he heaps the soil up high around the base of the plant.

The underground stems swell into new potatoes while the stems above ground produce flowers.

The potato is a food store, containing mostly starch. Just as the wood of a tree contains carbon from the air which has been processed in the leaves, so the starch of a potato contains processed carbon. This means that the quality of the potato depends on the condition of the leaves of the plant: they must be plentiful and healthy. For this reason, the gardener takes care that his plants are not affected by pests. He sprays them to protect them from insects which feed on the leaves until they wither. The larvae of the Colorado beetle, for example, are especially harmful to the potato plant. Spraying plus proper cultivation ensure a good crop of this vegetable which was once disregarded but is now so valuable a food.

The fruit of the potato plant

The Colorado beetle, an enemy of the plant

The potatoes are picked in fall when the plant has withered. The sturdiest ones will be kept to produce next year's crop.

The Swallows Return

The return of the swallows means that the winter really is over. In late April, the first ones skim in over the rooftops on the last stage of their journey home. A few days later larger numbers of them come flying in.

In the country, they are made welcome. No one has disturbed the rows of nests built by last year's swallows: they are valued friends and no one would think of destroying their homes. Many of their nests are lodged above doorways, often in a cowshed or stable. The birds manage to find their way through a stable door or a skylight and make themselves at home with the animals.

In town, especially in the big cities, it is a different story. Often the swallows cannot find their way about when they return: perhaps a new building has been erected on the spot where last year's nest was built, or an old house which once sheltered families of birds has been demolished. Each year there are fewer trees, food is more difficult to find and the noise gets worse. The birds can no longer fly through empty streets in the late evening.

As soon as the swallows arrive, they set to work to repair an old nest or build a new one. They are in a hurry to lay their eggs and rear the young birds who will have to be strong enough to make the long flight to warmer climates in the autumn. They collect bits of soil, animal hair and fine straw which they mix together and grind into a kind of mortar; it is such an efficient material that the nest remains firmly fixed in its position under a beam. Swallows like to life in groups, so they build their nests in rows, like houses along a street.

The parent birds come and go continually once the eggs hatch. They don't pick food up from the ground. They snap little flies up with their short, pointed beaks as they fly. They bring the live flies back to the young birds whose wide-open beaks protrude from the narrow opening at the top of the nest. The young birds are well trained. Their droppings are not allowed to soil the nest but are dropped out over the edge. This is a very inconvenient habit in town, but in the country it provides extra manure for the soil.

Swallows are superb acrobats. A quick flick of a wing and they wheel off on a completely different course. They are built for such agility. Like all birds, they are very light: they are heavier than air, of course, but their bones are porous, like a sponge, so that they weigh relatively little. The swallow owes its power and skill to its very long wings, which are fixed to its strong breastbone. Its distinctive, forked tail is used for steering. It is usually in the evening that swallows take to the air in large numbers and treat their spectators to a display of flying that would put the best aerobatics team to shame.

As well known as the swallow, because it also lives close to people, is the house martin. In their shape and behavior the two birds resemble one another very closely, but they differ

color: the swallow has a blue sheen on its
ack, and its head and throat are chestnut-
rown, whereas the house martin is black and
hite.

The swifts are seen less often because they
e most likely to haunt towers and belfries.
hey are bigger birds with long narrow wings
d are such expert fliers that they can even
eep on the wing. As they wheel and dip in
rsuit of one another, they let out piercing
rieks. But even these aggressive, noisy birds
e welcome, for they, too, are a sign that sum-
er is coming.

*Using mud and twigs, these swallows have built their nest in
a cowshed. This is the home they will return to each spring.*

MAY

More Migrants

Many other birds return to their summer homes in May after the swallows, but because they are not so numerous and remain more aloof, their arrival is not noticed so quickly.

In some European countries, storks arrive ahead of swallows. These big white birds have black-edged wings with a span of eight feet. They generally live in marshy areas because they feed on reptiles, amphibians and small rodents. Occasionally they make their homes in built-up places, balancing their nests like hats on top of disused chimneys. Their call is made by clacking their long beaks, and it sounds more like castanets than a bird song.

Cranes, too, make for the marshes, swooping across the sky in a V formation. When they are ready to take off again, they rear themselves up on their long thin legs and unfold their large wings.

The brown and gray turtle doves trave in flocks, but, once home, they split up into pairs. The two birds call to each other with melodious purring sound, called cooing. The ring doves, or wood pigeons, many of which do not migrate in winter, are like the turtle doves but they have reddish tints on the breast and white mark on the neck. They live constantly under the threat of the gun: pigeon is a popular ingredient of game pie in Europe.

Quails are threatened in the same way, but they still travel long distances to return each summer. They are squat birds with weak looking legs and a stumpy tail, quite the opposite of the sleek and powerful swallow, but the

In the marshes, a heron watches a flock of wild ducks take to the air.

till have plenty of energy. When they come
o rest after a flight, they immediately set off
gain at a run on their little legs. They usu-
lly take to the air again at dusk in search of
ying insects, or else they feed by pecking at
eeds and shoots on the ground.

Many wild ducks or mallards stay in the
me area all year, but some leave for the win-
r. They move about from place to place more
an most birds, flying overhead with their
ecks stretched forward and their legs drawn
ack under their tails to make them as stream-
ned as possible. As they prepare to land, they
wer their webbed feet and skate to a halt
er the surface of the water. The female
ilds her nest in a field, or at the water's edge,
in an old tree trunk, and there she lays five
six greenish-colored eggs. She stays in the
me place just long enough to rear her young
d to teach them to fly, and then she is on the

move again. It is amusing to watch a group of
ducks bobbing about on the water. Suddenly,
as if on order, they all dip their beaks into the
water to search for larvae or mollusks, and all
the tails stick straight up into the air. Then, just
as suddenly, the heads bob up again and the
ducks swim sedately on their way.

Herons also live together in groups, but they
keep their distance from people. They perch
their big nests of sticks high in old trees or on
cliffs.

A heron can sometimes be seen standing
in shallow water, watching for fish or small
animals: its sharp beak and long neck are
drawn back while it waits, but they flash out
quickly to seize a victim.

Many smaller birds return at the same time
as these more flamboyant ones: warblers, night-
ingales and others all add to the pleasures of
summer with their tuneful songs.

The gardener plants five or six beans around the base of each pole.

MAY

Planting Beans

The gardener is ready to plant his beans. He opens a wrinkled pod and takes out half a dozen beans. They are hard and white and round, like little pebbles.

If one of these little pebbles were left overnight in water to soak, by morning it would be moist and swollen, and it would look much more alive.

The skin of a bean (the tegument) is hard and no water can pass through it, but on one si of it, above a dark scar called the hilum, is small hole that lets air and water in. Wrapp in the tegument are the two main parts of t bean, the cotyledons. Small vessels, the ne vures, show through the tegument like vei under the skin.

Attached to one of the cotyledons and san wiched between them for safety is the embr

ean plant. It is a complete plant in its own
ght, but because it is so small, the names of
l its parts have special endings which indicate
s small size. Its root is called the radicle and
s shoot is the plumule.

The gardener plants his beans in the ground,
nd after a few days, they begin to grow.

If you would like to find out what happens
nderground, put a bean on wet cotton wool
d then watch it as it begins to grow. Almost
once the radicle appears from the little hole
ove the hilum and embeds itself in the cotton
ol.

Secondary roots soon branch out from the
ain one. The tip of each root is hard so that it
n push its way through the ground after the
an is planted, and above the tip are fine ab-
rbent root hairs through which the plant
n draw food from the soil.

Once the root is firmly established, the tegu-
ent splits open and, if the bean has been
anted, the first leaves rise up out of the
ound. In some plants these are the cotyle-
ns. They gradually turn green and separate,
owing the leaves of the plant to emerge. It
ows taller and straightens, and more leaves
velop. The new plant has used up the supply
food stored in the cotyledons by last year's
ant and is now strong enough to live inde-
ndently. The cotyledons wither.

The new plant will produce flowers and then
ds: green beans. If the pods are not picked
t are left to mature and ripen, bean seeds
dy for the following spring will develop in-
them.

One bean seed yields hundreds more, so
en though large quantities of beans are eaten,
re are still plenty left to produce the next
r's crop.

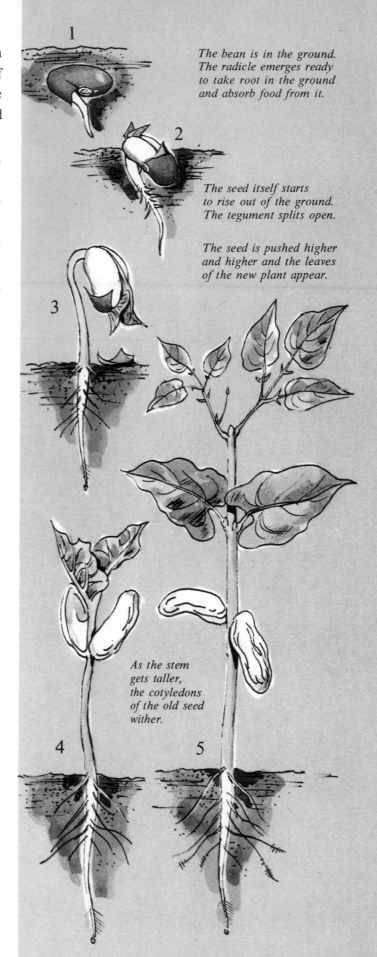

1

*The bean is in the ground.
The radicle emerges ready
to take root in the ground
and absorb food from it.*

2

*The seed itself starts
to rise out of the ground.
The tegument splits open.*

*The seed is pushed higher
and higher and the leaves
of the new plant appear.*

3

*As the stem
gets taller,
the cotyledons
of the old seed
wither.*

4   5

The Law of Nature

Everything in nature is very fertile. One bean seed multiplies into dozens of beans, each of which in its turn produces dozens more. Thousands of buds ripen on the chestnut trees, and there would soon be a forest where one tree had stood if each bud were allowed to complete its full cycle. If each frog's or toad's egg laid in the pond were to develop, the pond would not be large enough to hold all the new amphibians. If all the eels' eggs were to become mature fish, the vast ocean would soon become one big basket of eels. One cherry tree could provide thousands more of its kind.

The same goes for everything, plants or animals. The world would soon be overrun and overgrown if there were no controls, but just as everything reproduces itself naturally, so there are natural restraints on this reproduction.

Man controls the spread of cherry trees by eating their fruit, and blackbirds and starlings help him. The grosbeak follows and collects the discarded stones, cracks them in his large beak and eats the kernels. Squirrels do similar work in the woods, where they also devour acorns and beechnuts. The reproduction of all plants and animals is restricted in some way: the young are eaten by other creatures or destroyed by drought or frost.

The cruelty of this law of nature has to be recognized: all living things, and even minerals as well, are caught up in this pattern of mutual destruction. The ant gnaws the tree, the toad eats the ant, the snake eats the toad, the hedgehog eats the snake, the badger eats the hedgehog and so on. You would imagine that the last one in the line would be man, and that he would be safe from attack, but he in his turn can be destroyed by the smallest creature of all, the germs that continually threaten him. All nature seems to be a battlefield where everything has to struggle to survive; the principle at work everywhere is the survival of the fittest.

Only one of nature's creatures could alter this law, and that is man. While all the others must follow their instincts, man is in a position to master his own instincts and control those of others. He could make nature's law less cruel by protecting the weakest and so making sure

each species has its place on earth. Unfortunately, he rarely acts in this way and is often himself a destroyer. He destroys when he uses poison to get rid of harmful insects, forgetting that he is also poisoning the birds which feed on those insects. He destroys when he hunts down wild animals, and in this case he is sometimes doing it not from necessity but simply for his own pleasure.

Man does not always destroy; he has, for instance, established wildlife parks and nature reserves where all living things are protected. Now it is up to him to respect life outside the parks as well, except in cases where his own life is threatened. To destroy for pleasure is to behave more savagely than any animal. To continue doing so could slowly turn the world into a barren desert.

In the picture at the top of the page, a helicopter sprays insecticide on crops, killing birds along with the insects.

The picture on the facing page illustrates the struggle for survival. Man upsets the balance and is more cruel than the law of nature when he destroys for no purpose.

With the establishment of nature reserves, it is hoped that many species of animals now in danger of extinction will be preserved and allowed to live naturally; destruction will still go on but it will be according to the law of nature, to preserve the essential balance.

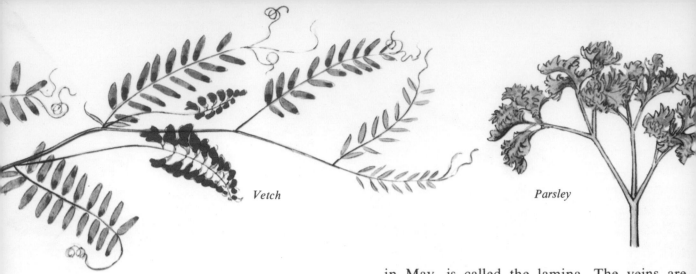

Vetch

Parsley

MAY

Leaves

When people walk in the country, they pick bluebells, violets or buttercups. When they are in the garden, they admire azaleas, irises and lilac. They rarely pause to look at one of the wonders of the plant world: the leaf. Even the name shows the extent to which it is disregarded. Flowers have different names, but all the different leaves are lumped together without any special names of their own.

People take a real interest in leaves only when they are thinking about food: lettuce or spinach, for instance. Yet leaves come in so many different shapes and sizes that they are a fascinating subject. The parsley leaf is an open hand; the rhubarb leaf is a big plate; boxwood leaves are like little coins; the pine leaf is a needle. Some leaves are simple, like those of the lilac, cherry, plum and apple. Others are made up of several leaflets, like those of the rose and the potato. The variety is endless.

The best way to examine the structure of a leaf is to pick up a dead one first: the "skin" crumbles away and exposes a network of fine veins. The "skin," green and full of chlorophyll

in May, is called the lamina. The veins are vessels through which the sap circulates.

The top of the lamina is quite different from the underside. The shiny top always faces the sun and all the chlorophyll is concentrated there. Chlorophyll is sensitive to sunlight in almost the same way that photographic film is. In sunlight, it acts as the catalyst in photosynthesis, the process by which the leaf manufactures sugar from carbon dioxide and water. This is the vital function of chlorophyll. Photosynthesis cannot occur at night when there is no light, or in winter when the leaves have fallen.

The underside of the leaf is dull and grayish. It is covered with little holes which behave like the pores in human skin. They allow plants to take in carbon dioxide and to "sweat"; the "sweating" of plants is called transpiration. From the ground, plants take in mineral salts dissolved in water and they discard excess water as vapor through the pores. They also need to get rid of excess heat, just as human beings do, and the evaporating water causes some cooling.

These pores also serve another purpose: they absorb very small quantities of oxygen from the air to enable the plant to "burn up" its food. This combustion is so slow that it does not give off heat, but a small amount of carbon dioxide is released through the pores. A sort of respiration, similar to human breathing, takes place in the plant.

The three activities of plants mentioned above, photosynthesis, transpiration and respiration, demonstrate that the plants are living things. Plants also have circulation. Moisture is absorbed by the roots and sap and then travels up to the leaves and through the vessels in the leaf, carrying nourishment to all parts of the plant; some of the moisture then returns to the roots again.

Apart from their method of building up their own food, there is only one thing that prevents plants from being classed as primitive animals along with sea anemones, sponges and corals, and that is the absence of a nervous system. It is through its nervous system that an animal reacts to changes in its surroundings. Although plants respond to their surroundings, they have no nervous system. The most that can be said is that certain sensitive plants contract when they are touched.

These leaves in their varied shapes are not just decorative. Plants depend on their leaves for respiration, transpiration and especially for their nourishment.

Iris

Horse chestnut

Pine

Poplar

Boxwood

Tansy

Ivy

71

At night a slow procession of snails makes its way toward some delicious lettuces.

MAY

Snails: The Silent Burglars

One day the lettuces in the garden look green and juicy, the next their leaves are in shreds. Burglars must have come in the night and ransacked the garden—clever, silent burglars.

But their tracks give them away. A silvery trail leads to two big stones. Beside them is a gray ball which looks too neatly rounded to be a pebble. It is stuck to the ground and is very difficult to pick up. When it does give way, it turns out to be a snail, which, in its fright, has withdrawn into its shell. This is the thief.

If he is returned to the lettuce patch, he remains motionless at first. After a while he gets braver; he puts out a foot and stretches his head upward. His shell still protects such vulnerable and important organs as his heart, liver and lungs.

There are still a few lettuce leaves left intact, and as the snail makes for them, it is easy to see the two pairs of horns, or antennae, on his head. The bigger pair have knobs at the end with black spots on them. These black spots are eyes, and since the antennae are mobile, they can look in different directions like a submarine's periscope. If an eye is cut off, the snail can grow another one; that is one advantage of being a simple animal. The two smaller antennae are the snail's "hands"; he touches and feels with them.

The antennae quickly detect a tasty lettuce leaf and the snail's powerful jaws come into play. If the garden is quiet, you can actually hear the munching. The snail also uses his file-like tongue with its 10,000 teeth. These teeth can never wear down because they keep on growing all the time. The lettuce leaf is crushed and ground between the teeth and the upper jaw; it disappears with amazing speed.

But even with such a good appetite, one snail could not wreck an entire lettuce patch in one night. Clinging to another leaf is a fat slug. It is as long as a finger and its striped skin is wrinkled. Like the snail, it has two pairs of antennae which function in the same way. Also, both creatures have a gland near the mouth which produces slime that allows them to move by sliding (the opening from this gland is easier to see on the slug than on the snail). The slime even allows these creatures to scale a wall or a tree trunk or occasionally to hang from a thread like a spider.

Behind the antennae is an opening through which eggs are laid. Slugs and snails lay their eggs into a hole which they have prepared in the ground. You come across them sometimes in summer with their heads deep in a hole, laying dozens of eggs. The young creep out of the hole a month later. Each year they grow larger, and another ring of calcium is added to the edge of the snails' shells. Snails and slugs can

live to be eight years old if they manage to escape the attentions of man, amphibians, hedgehogs, moles, birds and beetles.

They are cold-blooded, so they go to sleep as soon as winter threatens and do not wake up until the sun is really hot and the lettuces are ready to satisfy their hearty appetites. But if food is short, they can survive quite a long fast.

They have no interior skeleton, so they are invertebrates. They are mollusks, creatures which have a soft body that is usually protected by a calcium shell. There are mollusks in the sea, too.

Slugs and snails have jaws and a hard, horny tongue. On the head are two pairs of antennae, the larger pair bearing eyes. Both animals lay their eggs through an opening behind the antennae into a hole in the ground, and the young emerge about a month later.

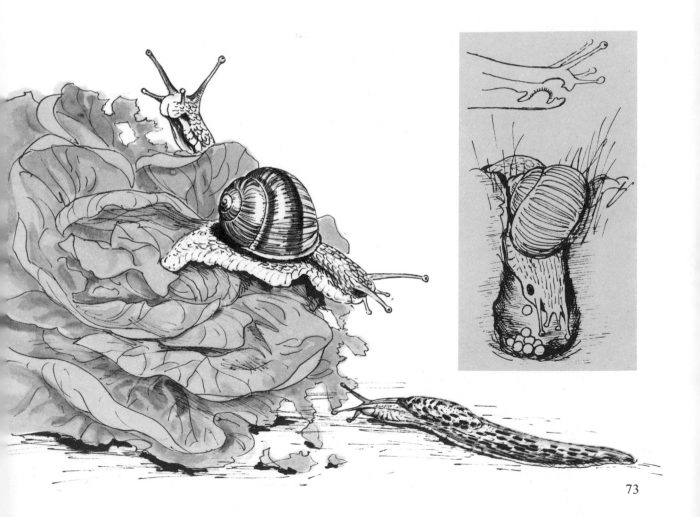

Lilies of the valley

Flowers of the Fields and Woods

"April showers bring May flowers" is an old saying, and it is true that by the first of May many flowers are appearing in the gardens and in the woods and fields. The lilies of the valley are out now in the gardens, although in the woods, where there is more shade, they flower a little later. Lilies of the valley grow from an underground stem like potatoes, but there are no tubers. Swellings appear at intervals along the underground stem (the rhizome) and these become buds. The buds open into leaves and slender stems bearing white bell-shaped flowers with a delicate perfume.

The wood hyacinth with its small, blue bell-shaped flowers is carpeting the woods so that from a distance they look quite blue. The common name of the wood hyacinth is the bluebell.

The primrose grows best in shady places in fairly heavy moist soil. Its pale yellow petals and delicate scent make it a favorite wild flower. The primrose belongs to the family of the Primula, as does the cowslip.

In shaded corners of the woods and field violets are growing close to the ground. The flowers grow singly on slender stalks and their five petals are different in size; the lowest one is much larger than the others. The violet much-loved for its sweet scent.

The small flowers of the wild forget-me-not can also be found growing in the fields and hedges. It has a softly hairy stem and light green leaves. The flower buds are pink, but become blue as the flowers open.

The hawthorn trees are covered in pink or white flowers. The flowers are full of nectar and pollen for the bees but they are well protected by sharp thorns on the stem of the tree. In autumn they turn into red berries, called haws, a favorite food of birds.

The fields are full of daisies shining white against the dark grass. Their name means "day's eye" because the petals unfold in the morning and close up again at night. The daisy belongs to the family of flowers called Compositae because each flowerhead is composed of many tiny flowers. Arranged round the swollen end of the stem are hundreds of yellow tubes which form the heart of the flower; each tube is a flower in its own right, made up of five petals joined together, with stamens and a stigma inside. Ringing the yellow center are more flowers, including a coronet of petals that are much larger and white, and this is the part of the daisy that is usually noticed.

Among the daisies is a lovely golden flower which is usually ignored, except by children who collect its leaves as a treat for their pet rabbits: the dandelion. It also belongs to the family of the Compositae but the flower does not have the distinctive center; all the tubes that make up the dandelion flower have one long extended petal, so it is a much fuller flower than the daisy. In autumn, when each tiny flower on the flowerhead has been fertilized and has produced its seed, the dandelion is a pompon of fine down which, when blown, is scattered on the wind. The seeds float on their "parachutes" to new spots where dandelions will spring up next year.

Daisy

Forget-me-not

Dandelion

Haymaking

While the warm June sun is shining, the farmer is already thinking about the cold days of winter, even though they are still a long way off. He climbs on his mowing machine and sets off for the meadow; it is not a natural meadow where wild grasses grow freely, but an artificial one, which next year will be ploughed and prepared for a crop of corn or beets.

In the meadow the ground is thickly covered. Clusters of purple flowers color the surface. These are the flowers of the alfalfa, which has clover-like leaves and produces a pod like that of the pea, but smaller. Because it produces this pod, it belongs, like the clover, to the family of leguminous plants. The plant is cut when it is in full flower and before it has yielded its fruit.

The alfalfa (below left) and the clover (right) are leguminous plants. After haymaking, they are dried and used to enrich the hay the animals will feed on through the winter

The alfalfa falls to the ground, swollen with sap. During the long warm days it will be left to wilt and dry. This is how animal fodder is prepared. The leaves and flowers will go crisp but will still retain their flavor. When they are ready, they will be stored away in the haystack as a reserve food for the animals in winter.

The alfalfa is not the only plant used for animal fodder. Different types of clovers (the red clover and the white clover), with their ball-shaped flowerheads, are used for some artificial meadows. Others are sown with sainfoin; its pink flowers grow in spikes.

In summer, the animals are not allowed to graze in the artificial meadows. The vegetation there is too rich and plentiful and would make them ill. Instead, they spend the fine weather grazing on natural pasture.

The natural meadow is the home of the grasses. These are often not sown by man but

grown naturally among other plants, if soil and climate are suitable. Grass is a very vague term; the family name Gramineae, though it includes several thousands of different plants, is more accurate.

The Gramineae are plants with long stems. The flowers grow in a spike at the top of the stem, sometimes loosely grouped together, sometimes tightly packed. There are hundreds of kinds of Gramineae, including foxtail, wild oats, fescue, and meadow grass.

Like the leguminous plants of the artificial meadows, the Gramineae of the natural meadows are also cut and dried and then stored ready for the winter. That is what is usually meant by hay.

Throughout the summer, the cows feed on the natural grass in the fields. They graze. But even when they are not actually cropping the grass, their jaws move continuously. This is part of the very elaborate process of changing grass into milk inside the cow.

First the grass is swallowed, almost without being chewed. It goes into the cow's enormous paunch, which can store more than 175 quarts! From there it passes into the cow's second stomach (the reticulum) and, once thoroughly mixed with the digestive juices stored there, it is regurgitated into the mouth to be ground down and mixed with saliva. From the mouth, it returns to be processed in the large folds of the third stomach (the omasum) and then in the finer folds of the fourth stomach (known as the abomasum). The final stages of the transformation and digestion take place in the small intestine.

The cow is a marvelous natural machine. Nothing invented by man can process grass reaped in June and provide milk all the year round.

The Fish

The fish, unlike the amphibian, can live only in the water. Its body is at the same temperature as the water, but each kind of fish can live only within certain limits. There are warm-water fish and cold-water fish. The temperature of the water affects egg-laying and reproduction. The perch will lay eggs only in a temperature of about 57°F, while the carp needs over 68°F.

Although fish live in water, they still need oxygen from the air. They can get it because water contains dissolved air. Water enters the body of the fish through the mouth, which opens and closes continuously. It then passes over the gills; these are like rows of combs, and they look red because blood is always circulating through them. In the gills oxygen is extracted from the water and carbon dioxide passed back into the water, as in all forms of respiration. The water then flows away as the gill covers open and close. If the fish is taken out of water, it suffocates, because the only air available is not in the form it can breathe.

Some of the air that is taken from the water is kept in a bag inside the fish's body. This bag is called the air bladder, or swim bladder, and it is a very efficient buoy. There is usually just enough air in this bladder to enable the fish to float weightlessly like a balloon. If the fish needs more or less buoyancy, the amount of air in the bladder can be changed slowly.

Fish, especially the flesh-eating, or carnivorous, ones, have more teeth than any other animals. There are teeth in the jaws, the palate and even the pharynx (the upper part of the gullet), and some of them are very sharp.

The fish has a skeleton with a backbone and has a long body with two sides, so it is classed as a vertebrate, although a rather simple one. Only animals without a backbone (invertebrates) are lower down the scale of development. The amphibians are immediately above the fish because they have limbs, whereas the fish has to use fins to make its way through the water. The pectoral fins replace arms and the pelvic fins replace legs. The fins on its back (dorsal) and at the rear underside (anal) usually provide stability, and the tail, or caudal, fin drives the fish through the water.

The fish's big spherical eyes stand out clearly because they have no eyelids. Less noticeable, but very useful for the fish, is a line which runs along each side of the body. Known as the lateral line, it consists of a row of tiny openings containing nerve fibers which are sensitive to pressure changes in the surrounding water and so warn the fish of possible danger.

The skin of the fish is worth a close look. It often has a rainbow-tinted sheen, with glints of silver and gold, and this hard "metallic" coat is made of scales which are cleverly laid, like roof tiles, so that the water flows over them without meeting any resistance.

Like its distant relations, the invertebrates and the amphibians, the fish usually lays eggs. Large numbers of them are stored in the body

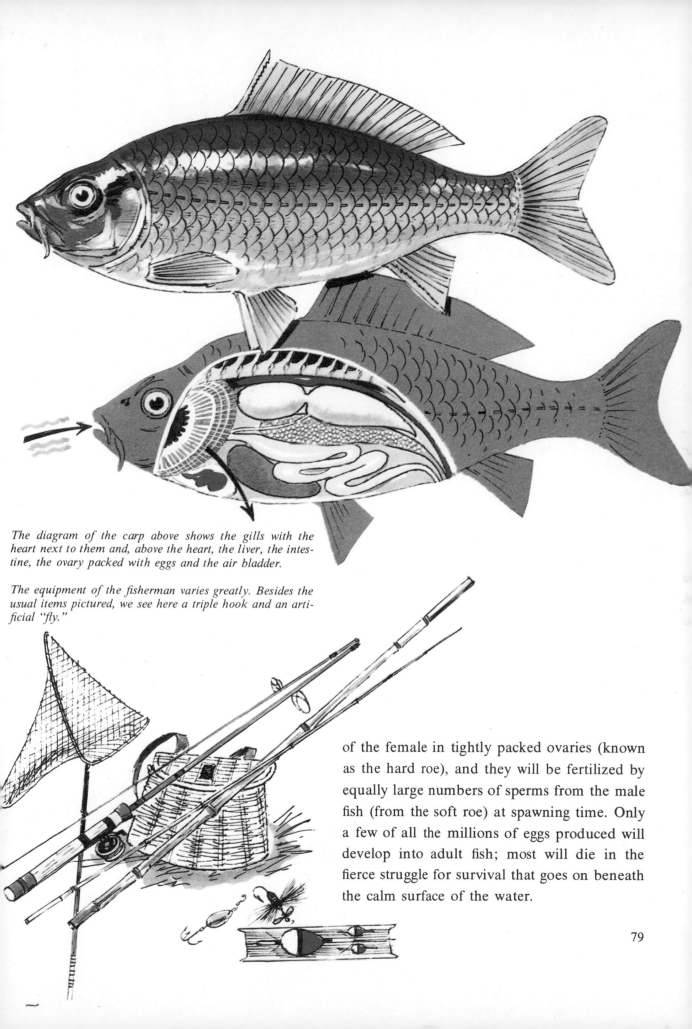

The diagram of the carp above shows the gills with the heart next to them and, above the heart, the liver, the intestine, the ovary packed with eggs and the air bladder.

The equipment of the fisherman varies greatly. Besides the usual items pictured, we see here a triple hook and an artificial "fly."

of the female in tightly packed ovaries (known as the hard roe), and they will be fertilized by equally large numbers of sperms from the male fish (from the soft roe) at spawning time. Only a few of all the millions of eggs produced will develop into adult fish; most will die in the fierce struggle for survival that goes on beneath the calm surface of the water.

79

JUNE

Freshwater Fish

To the lover of good food, the trout and the salmon are the first names that usually spring to mind when freshwater fish are mentioned. Both salmon and some trout are migratory fish which come into the rivers to lay their eggs. They choose clear, fast-flowing water, and they may sometimes be seen leaping up above the surface.

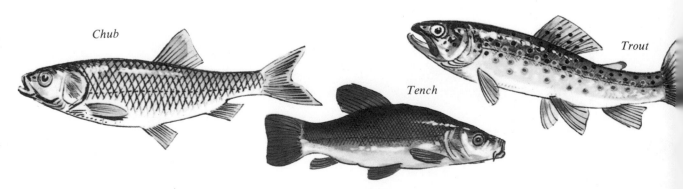

Chub

Tench

Trout

Less impressive fish inhabit the quieter streams.

The gudgeon is a small freshwater fish about 5 inches long. It has short dorsal and anal fins and a fleshy filament called a barbel hanging from each corner of its mouth. Its skin is shaded with yellow, brown and blue. Gudgeon move about in small shoals at this time of the year when they are spawning.

The bleak has a long anal fin and its scales are bright with a pearly substance that can be extracted and used for making synthetic pearls. It always seems to be pouting because its lower jaw sticks out beyond its upper jaw.

The minnow is good to eat fried. Its body is round rather than flat and has deep lines marked along its sides. It is greenish-blue in color with a pink or red belly.

There are bigger fish in the deeper water of the rivers. The chub can be 24 inches long and is sometimes easy to catch because it pounces greedily on almost any bait. Its back is grayish-purple, its sides and belly are silver and its fins are tinted red or green. Its scales are large and it has a forked tail.

The perch is just as greedy as the chub, but its favorite diet is small fish. It has two fins on its back very close together, and the front one is hard and spiny. The colors of the perch change according to the season and the locality in which it is found.

The catfish has a smooth, scaleless body, long barbels around the mouth, and spines in the dorsal and pectoral fins. Some catfish prefer clear, moving water; others live in muddy waters. Large-sized catfish are good for eating.

The tench prefers muddy ponds to running water. Its body is oval-shaped and covered with very small scales tinted green and bronze. Its head is thick and slimy and there is a barbel at each side of its mouth. It casts its skin from time to time and becomes a beautiful golden color splashed with black. It can grow to 20 inches in length and weigh 10 or 12 pounds.

The carp can weigh as much as 45 pounds. It has four barbels on the head and the female lays thousands of eggs.

The "shark" of freshwater fish is the pike, which controls the river population by preying on all kinds of fish, large and small. It waits motionless among the weeds until its victims swim by. The pike's voracity ensures that of all the thousands of eggs laid by the carp and the perch, only a few grow into adult fish. The body of the pike is long and slender, ideal for a predator, and its flattened mouth contains about 700 teeth. The pike is the big prize that many freshwater fishermen dream about.

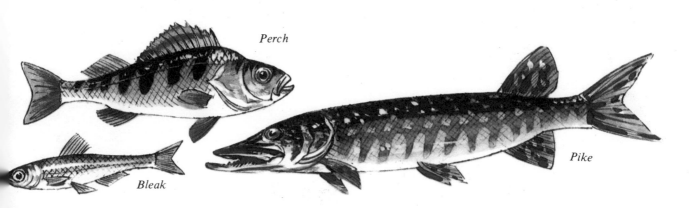

Perch

Bleak

Pike

81

SUMMER

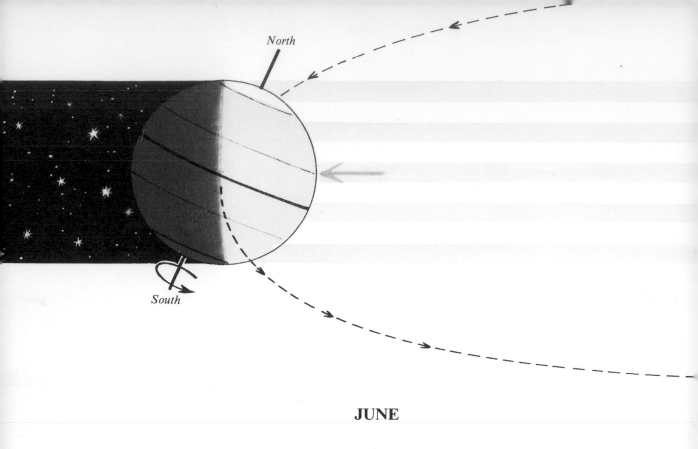

North

South

JUNE

Summer Solstice

Since the spring equinox, the Earth has continued its revolution round the sun. Viewed from the Earth, the sun has appeared to rise farther to the left and to set a little more to the right each day since Christmas. By June it is rising in the northeast and setting in the northwest. Only at midday does it always shine from

The Earth (above) has reached that point on its course around the sun where the North Pole and the Arctic Circle are lit for the full twenty-four hours. This day is therefore the longest day of the year in the Northern Hemisphere: the summer solstice.

The two solstices, summer and winter, are drawn below as they appear to someone looking from the Northern Hemisphere. At the time of the summer solstice the sun is high and the day is long; at the time of the winter solstice, the sun is low and the day is short.

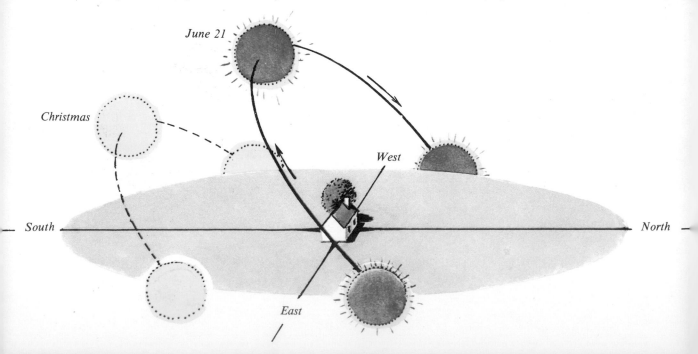

June 21

Christmas

West

South   North

East

In the Arctic Circle in summer the sun goes down at night but it never drops below the horizon. The result is continuous daylight in the middle of summer. Here we see a midnight scene in Lapland.

the same direction, the south, but in June it is much higher in the sky than before.

If this daily movement were to continue, the point where the sun rises and the point where it sets would eventually coincide, and the sun would make a complete circle in the sky. But this movement does not continue. It stops at the summer solstice, midsummer day, the longest day of the year. This is the day when the northern half of the globe, the Northern Hemisphere, has its longest period of light. Once it is past, the movement is reversed.

It is possible to see the sun complete a full circle in the sky, but not in the main part of the United States. You would have to go farther north—into northern Alaska, for instance. Since the spring equinox, the northern half of the globe has been leaning more and more toward the

sun until, on the day of the summer solstice, the sun lights up the whole of the polar region. Just by entering the Arctic Circle, at the northern tip of Norway, for instance, tourists can enjoy continuous daylight in the middle of the summer.

Not many people, however, find the polar region a very inviting prospect for vacations. They prefer a spot where the sun reaches its highest point, where it shines directly overhead at midday. On the day of the summer solstice this would be, not on the equator, but on the Tropic of Cancer, which is the hottest place in summer.

But wherever you choose to spend the summer, you can't entirely forget that midsummer day is the turning point from which the northern half of the Earth starts its gradual return to winter.

85

Garden Flowers

The garden is at its best in June. At the back of the border are the hollyhocks which sometimes reach a height of six feet or more. They have a spray of large flowers at the top of each stem. Some are single flowers, some are double, and they are usually pink in color.

As tall and straight as the hollyhocks are the sunflowers. Their name seems exactly right for them, because they are round and yellow and they always turn to face the sun. Each sunflower can measure as much as six to eight inches across.

The peony can be mistaken for a rose with its full pink or red flower, but each flower is supported by a straight slender stem without thorns.

Gladioli grow from bulbs planted in March and produce banks of flowers of all colors. They are the florist's favorites because they last for such a long time and because their colors are so varied.

The flower of the madonna lily is carried on a very fine stem and its petals are a brilliant white, except where a few grains of its abundant golden pollen have fallen onto them.

There are flowers belonging to the family of Compositae in the garden just as there are in the fields. The sunflower is one of them. Also related to the daisy is the aster, which has many different forms and colors. It came originally from China. Other flowers of the same family include the red or golden gaillardia and the lavender-blue ageratum. Orange marigolds, members of the Compositae family again, grow freely everywhere; in fact, they spread so rapidly that the gardener's problem is trying to keep them within bounds.

Climbing plants decorate walls and archways. The white, red or purple bells of the convolvulus close up at the sunniest time of the day. The orange or yellow flowers of the nasturtium droop to a point behind, like the hood on a monk's habit. The white and purple flowers of the clematis have velvety petals, but

though the plant produces stems each year, they do not always bear flowers. Sweet peas are very well named; the plant is closely related to the garden pea, and the flowers, which are of many different colors, have a very sweet and delicate scent.

A summer bouquet! Here you can see the delphinium, gladiolus, lupin, aster, rose, carnation, madonna lily, flag iris, clematis, veronica, marigold, nasturtium, poppy, anemone and campanula.

Along the edges of the flower beds there are purple campanulas. Behind them are the clear, fresh colors of the bright geraniums and the brilliant yellows and russets of the sweet-scented wallflowers.

Even leaves add their colors to the splendid show: the coleus, or flame nettle, has variegated leaves, each one with patches of different colors ranging from green and yellow through to copper-tinted red and purple.

Cereals

The ancient Romans believed that the gods and goddesses watched over everything that was important to them; mountains, rivers, forests and the sea all had their own gods. The goddess who protected flowers, fruit and the harvest was called Ceres. Our word "cereals" comes from her name.

In July the cereals are still green. Scattered among them in the fields are scarlet poppies and cornflowers with jagged petals of a brilliant blue. All cereals are grasses, or Gramineae; they all have a long stem, which is usually hollow, and a leaf branching from each node, or bump, on the stem. At the top of the stem is a spike, or ear, full of edible starchy seeds. Wheat, rice and rye are cereals grown mainly for human food; maize, barley and oats are grown mostly for livestock.

Oats are different from other cereals. The spikelets hang on individual stems, producing a loosely formed spike, while the spikelets of the other cereals are clustered closely round the stem. Oats are fed to horses, and in some colder regions, where wheat does not ripen well, they are much used in family cooking, too. The fame of Scottish porridge and oatcakes has spread far beyond Scotland.

The ear of barley is covered by straw which extends into a long, whiskery beard. It is made up of scales, but they are not arranged alternately like those of wheat and rye; they are set in columns (either two or six) around the stem. Barley is used in stews and broths and also in the complicated process of brewing beer.

Each spikelet on rye has short whiskers. The stem of rye is taller and more pliable than that

Flowers of the fields: cornflower and poppy

Barley *Wheat* *Oats* *Rye*

f wheat. Even in places where wheat ripens ell, rye is sometimes also grown since it akes good animal fodder if it is cut before the uit forms. In poor ground, it will ripen where heat would not. The dark bread (called black read) which used to be the regular food of oor people in many countries was made of e. Nowadays, the present fashion for natural ealth foods has made rye bread popular ain.

Wheat is sometimes called the "king" of ceals. The ear of the wheat is made up of parate grains arranged alternately around the em. Each grain or kernel of wheat is covered by a thin shell often called the bran. This is removed by milling processes when the wheat is ripe. The top of each grain has a sharp point or sometimes hairs, though these are generally shorter than those of barley or rye.

Wheat is grown mainly for human food and the wheat grain is an important source of energy. It contains many vitamins and also a protein substance called gluten which is essential for making ordinary bread. Gluten is present only in wheat and, to a much smaller extent, in rye. It is the white flour from wheat that is the principal ingredient of most breads and other baked goods.

JULY

The Sea and the Tides

The land warms up quickly during the day and slowly loses its heat during the night. The sea, on the other hand, absorbs an enormous amount of heat from the sun into its huge volume of water but its temperature rises very slowly. Because of this, the sea modifies the effects of changes in the climate, and countries surrounded by sea do not suffer the extremes of cold and heat experienced in the center of great land masses.

Seven tenths of the surface of the Earth covered by sea, but scientists are only just beginning to understand it. It is known that there is life even in the darkest ocean depths, but there is still a lot to be learned about the sea.

Even the water itself is almost alive. It moves continuously. The waves rise and fall, building up from the horizon and crashing onto the shore. The wind whips them up higher and higher until they are sometimes sixty feet high.

Seawater also moves toward and away from the land. These movements are called tides. In an advance lasting six hours, the sea invades the shore, overrunning the beaches and filling the estuaries; this is the tide rising. Then there is a pause in the advance and this is called

At low tide huge expanses of sand are exposed and sea birds comb it for their food.

gh tide. For the next six hours the sea re-
ats; this is the tide ebbing. There is again a
use, which is called low tide, and then the
ter begins to flow forward again. These
vements never stop. About twice a month,
sea advances and goes out farther than
al: these bigger tides are called spring tides.
Tides are caused by the "pull" exerted on
Earth by the moon and the sun. Every
dy in space maintains its proper position in
ation to all the other bodies because of the
raction of one to another. The moon attracts
Earth but the Earth is held in position be-
se it also comes under the influence of the
raction of other bodies in space. The effect
the "pull" exerted by the moon on the Earth
scarcely noticeable on the land, but it has a
at influence on the sea because the sea is
uid. It causes the sea to ebb and flow as the

Earth rotates. Spring tides occur when the
moon and the sun are pulling together (at full
moon and new moon); neap tides (when there
is the least amount of tidal movement) occur
when the moon is pulling the waters in the
opposite direction to the sun (at the first and
third quarters of the moon).

Tides are also affected by the seasons. The
fullest tides of the year happen at the times of
the spring and fall equinoxes.

There is even "wind" in the sea. Just as cold
air moves in to replace rising warm air and
creates wind over the land, so there is a similar
movement in the sea as cold water from the
poles moves in deep down under the equator to
replace the water there which is warming up
and rising to the surface. This flow of water
forms currents. Currents are also affected by
the rotation of the Earth.

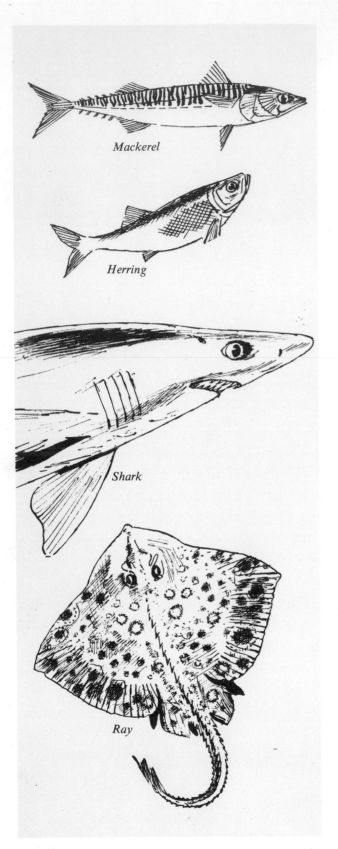

Mackerel

Herring

Shark

Ray

Sea Fish

The amount of water in a river—even one as long as the Mississippi or as wide as the Amazon—is minute compared with the enormous quantity stored in the seas and oceans. The ocean reaches a depth of over 6 miles in some places and stretches from the Arctic to the Antarctic (a distance of 12,000 miles). So it is not surprising that many millions of animals of all shapes and sizes inhabit the ocean; many of them, of course, are fish. They all produce as many young as freshwater fish do: hundreds of thousands or even millions, but as fish eat one another and as man goes on fishing for food, the ocean is never overpopulated.

On the contrary, it is feared that some species may even be dying out, but not for want of food. In fact, there is a vast and inexhaustible supply of nourishing "soup" floating on the top of the ocean; it measures about 100 yards in depth and spreads over a wide area. The "meat" content of this soup consists of all sorts of microscopic animals; they are nearly all transparent and some are luminous, too. The "vegetables" are microscopic plants which can live by the action of their chlorophyll, just as land plants do. It is the chlorophyll in the sea plants that gives the sea its blue-green colour. This "soup" is called plankton and the supply is inexhaustible because the organisms which compose it reproduce continuously. The fish eat as they swim along.

Representatives of all species of animals, from protozoa right up to mammals, inhabit the ocean. In the unfathomable depths there are monstrous fish living in total darkness and under a great weight of water. Some light their own way by means of mobile "lamps" on their bodies, and some have phosphorescent bodies. There are even electric fish in the sea: the electric ray and the electric eel can produce a discharge of electricity strong enough to paralyze or even kill a man.

But the best-known fish live nearer to the surface. They are the ones eaten by man.

Tuna fish are brought in by fishing boats from warm water. These fish can be as much as 17 feet long and can weigh a ton. They are the biggest fish caught regularly. They migrate, so boats follow the shoals on their journeys.

The ray is a striking fish because it has such a strange appearance. Its pectoral fins are so broad and thick that they form the largest part of its body. It can measure several yards across. It is a carnivorous fish and lives on the seabed, always on the lookout for prey. Its mouth is hidden on the underside of its body and its eyes are on top.

The mackerel is among the most beautiful fish on the fishmonger's slab; it is shiny green and blue, striped with black on the top side of its body and pearly-white on its underside.

The herring, like all fish that live in shoals, follows the movements of the plankton. There are millions of herring in a shoal, so they need a plentiful supply of food. They can make the sea sparkle when they swim by in such large numbers. It is a wonderful sight for the fisherman. He is equally delighted if he comes upon a shoal of sardines on their seasonal migration.

Cod comes from Newfoundland and Iceland. These fish come down from the polar regions to look for food and are caught at the spot where the cold and warm currents meet and the plankton collects in a huge mass.

One of the interesting events of a holiday by the sea is the return of the fishing boats. This long-finned tuna has been thrown up on the dock.

In the Mountains

The cool freshness that people long for during a heat wave can be found in the mountains, which makes them fine places for vacations. The deeper you go down below ground, the hotter it becomes—and conversely, the higher you go, the cooler it becomes. So you can enjoy whatever temperature suits you best just by climbing a mountain and stopping at the appropriate height.

Up to a height of 500 or 600 yards, the climate is the same as it is on the plain except that the nights are a little cooler. For this reason, the crops are also the same: wheat, oats, corn, grapes, apples and pears. Beyond this level few crops can grow because there are night frosts from August to May. Forests of beech and oak grow at this height. Higher still, these trees give way to conifers, which are more resistant to cold partly because their needles are less affected by low temperatures than our ordinary leaves. Here, the forests of larch and fir trees are silent.

In the region just below the snow line even these hardy trees cannot survive. There is just the odd fir tree, stunted and twisted by storms and high winds. The only form of vegetation at this level is grass. When the thaw comes, the grass drinks in the melting snow and grows very rapidly in the full summer sun. It provides excellent pasture for cattle and sheep. In the Swiss Alps, for instance, the cowherds and shepherds lead their animals up the mountains to graze throughout the summer. The men may be away from the farm for four or five months, living a very lonely life but enjoying the splendid views of mountains and sky.

Beyond the grass there is only rock and endless snow, right up to the summit of the mountain. In the mountains of southern Europe and southwestern Asia, this is the home of the chamois, a small goat-like antelope, and the wild goat. The snow is permanent. Loose new snow does not rest for long on the sheer rock faces but falls into the rocky clefts and ravines. As it collects there, it changes from soft airy particles into hard compact granules; in this state it is known as firn. Pressure exerted by succeeding layers of snow soon turns the firn into ice and it is now part of a glacier, a river of ice which stretches along the ravine from the mountain peak down to the line where the temperature is high enough to melt it. A glacier looks motionless but it is actually moving all the time, at the rate of several feet per year. It moves partly because of the pull of gravity and partly because the weight of the ice at the surface crushes the lower layers, causing them to disintegrate and slide imperceptibly downward. This movement deep within the glacier causes the surface to split and buckle, forming cre-

In the European Alps, one must climb very high, to pastures at the foot of the glaciers, to find (left) the chamois, grouse, marmot, edelweiss, and eagle. When the snow melts high in the mountains, the grass grows quickly, providing excellent pasture for cattle and sheep (below).

vasses. These are very dangerous to mountaineers, especially when they are bridged by a thin layer of newly fallen snow.

As the glacier moves, it wears away the rock beneath it and on its sides, and carries chunks of broken rock along with it. When it reaches the point on the mountain where the temperature is high enough to melt the ice into a gushing stream, the rocks are left behind and form a pile of debris known as a moraine.

The mountaineer can climb up through these different areas, or zones, each with their different climates but he has to be well trained and properly equipped. The air high up in the mountains is thin, and heart and lungs soon suffer from a shortage of oxygen without special breathing equipment. The wise amateur calls a halt at the halfway stage, at a spot where the air is clear and cool and the surroundings are bright and attractive.

Bread

The story of bread starts with wheat, but not wheat as we know it today. A long time ago, wheat was just a wild grass and could not produce the fat, flour-rich grain of today. By careful selection, only the best seeds from this poor wheat were preserved each year and sown to produce the next year's crop, until gradually the quality of the grain improved. After long years of such selection and experimentation, the strains of wheat available to the farmer today are of very high quality, but research still continues to enable farmers to produce the best possible crop under many different conditions.

Once good seeds have been selected, work starts on preparing the ground for sowing.

Machines have made this work easier, but it is still very demanding. The work starts as soon as the previous year's harvest is cleared. First the ground is ploughed in long furrows. Then when it has dried out after the autumn rains harrowing makes it soft and light; now it is ready for the seeds to be sown. The farmer uses a seed-drill for this job. The seeds remain dormant underground through the winter, protected from the frost at certain times by a covering of snow; in spring frail shoots appear. To make sure the roots are firmly established, and also to encourage them to produce more than one stem each, the farmer uses a rolling machine to flatten the tiny shoots back into the

96

Bread is the product of sun and rain and hard work on the part of many people. The gradual introduction of the machine has made man's job much easier. The picture shows a combine harvester at work.

ound. When new shoots appear again, they ust be protected from disease and encroach- g weeds and given extra nourishment if they m weak.

By the end of the summer, provided that gh winds haven't flattened the wheat and cessive rain hasn't turned it moldy, it is ready be harvested. On large farms the wheat is eshed as it is cut. On smaller farms it is tied o sheaves and left standing in stocks to dry t before being taken into the barn, or it may stored in a stack in the field; it will be eshed later.

Once the harvest is in, the most demanding t of the farmer's job is over, but he still has protect the grain from damp, parasites, insects d field mice, to clean it of loose soil and to

sift out any grains of inferior quality. At last it is ready to be sent off to the mill. It is ground by millstones, and the miller separates out the husks, or chaff, and sifts the flour.

The flour goes from the mill to the bakery where the baker is at work before dawn, kneading the dough, weighing out yeast and watching over the ovens to produce an appetizing batch of loaves. Still warm from the ovens, the crusty loaves reach the shelves of the baker's shop. Perhaps if the baker's customers knew something of the effort required to produce the bread, they would enjoy eating it all the more.

AUGUST

Summer Storms

August can produce periods of intense heat. As the heat builds up from day to day, the air becomes heavy and oppressive; everyone feels that a storm is threatening. Toward evening the horizon darkens, black clouds gather overhead, and sudden gusts of wind shake the trees and set the dust swirling.

Suddenly there is a flash of lightning. The heat of the sun has created a lot of electricity in the atmosphere. A powerful electric charge can be carried by a cloud, and if this comes too close to the ground, with so much electricity present, the result is the same as if two live electric wires suddenly touch each other; there

is a tremendous spark. This is lightning. It m be several miles in length and have a charge millions of volts. It can prove fatal to anyone the vicinity. It strikes at the highest points any area. That is why taking shelter under tree is foolish. Since a tree is probably one the highest points in a stretch of open land, i particularly likely to be struck. Lightning c set fire to haystacks or houses. In an attempt safeguard life and property, it is usual to ins a lightning conductor on a high building sor where—a church steeple, for instance. This a metal rod or wire fixed to an exposed part the building which carries the lightning into ground, allowing the electricity to flow av harmlessly.

Shortly after the flash of lightning th comes a sound like a roll of drums amplifie thousand times—the thunder. Light travels a speed of 186,300 miles per second, so ve sees lightning almost as soon as it flashes. ound travels much less quickly, at a speed of 70 yards per second, so it registers on the ear short time later. By counting the number of conds between the flash of the lightning and e roll of the thunder, it is possible to calcu- te how far away the lightning occurred. If ten conds elapse, then the cyc of the storm is 700 yards away (370 × 10). (If five seconds apse, the storm is about a mile away.)

It is a relief when the worst of the storm sses and the sun comes out again. Often a agnificent rainbow appears in the sky. This ppens because the rays of the sun filter rough the falling rain. The white light of the n is broken up by the raindrops into seven lors: red, orange, yellow, green, blue, indigo d violet. (The same effect can be seen by tching sunlight falling on a crystal glass or se.) These are basic colors which cannot be lit up any further. The most important are ue, green and red. Different combinations of

these colors produce, for example, the whole range of shades in a color television picture.

In some parts of the world, the heat is so in- tense at the height of summer that the hot air rises in a spiral. Trees, houses and even ships are caught up in this whirlwind. It is called a cyclone. Recent systems introduced to warn of the approach of a cyclone enable people to take cover, but there is little these warnings can do to prevent severe damage.

When summer reaches its peak in August, the heat of the sun sometimes becomes oppres- sive. Sunshine then is not always welcomed quite so eagerly as it was in the first mild days of spring, and the inhabitants of many coun- tries, especially in the tropics, seek shade in the middle of the day.

The summer sky darkens and lightning flashes on the hori- zon. As the rain eases off after the storm, the rainbow ap- pears, an arc of seven colors. Lightning can destroy: the tree in the picture below (left) has been struck by lightning. The picture on the right shows how a lightning conductor attracts lightning and carries it harmlessly into the ground.

AUGUST

Nocturnal Creatures

The warm nights of August are the best time to see some of the creatures called nocturnal; they sleep during the day and come out after dark. It is best to find a quiet place in the country and to wait there, watching and listening.

Dark shapes flit by overhead. They move so fast that they are difficult to identify. They are too big for insects, and the way they move their wings suggests they may be birds. But the strange creature that moved its wings like a bird is suckling a baby as it flies; that means that it must be some sort of mammal. It is one of nature's surprises, a flying mammal: a bat.

Like other mammals, bats have four limbs. The hind ones have claws which hook onto a rafter or the roof of a cave when the bat hibernates. It sleeps through the winter upside down, with its wings folded, safely hooked up out of sight. The forelimbs each consist of a short upper arm, a longer forearm and a hand with very elongated fingers. A thin layer of skin, without feathers, links the fingers and stretches across both limbs to form wings.

The bat has a full set of teeth; it also has eyes, but these are very inefficient. Since it lives in the dark, the bat needs a special system of detection. Therefore it has a sort of radar—a special organ which sends out very high-pitched sound waves which bounce back from objects and warn the bat of approaching danger or obstacles in its path.

So our first creature of the night was not a bird, after all! But there are birds that are active at night: these are the owls. Even when the keep out of sight, owls announce themselves b hooting or screeching. They are birds of pre with hooked beaks, four powerful claws, o talons, on each leg, large round yellow eye and acute powers of hearing. Their feathers ar thick and soft, especially those on the wing so they fly silently. They prey on rodents, a kinds of mice, moles, and young rabbits.

Parent owls look after their young very care fully, feeding, grooming and defending then but as soon as the young birds are old enoug to take on these tasks themselves, they leav the parents' nest to live independently. Fro then on, they count as strangers and would t chased off like any other intruder if they we to return to their parents' territory.

All owls have the same distinctive facial fe tures: large forward-looking eyes on either si of the short, hooked beak and a circular a rangement of feathers which accentuates t eyes. The barn owl, as its name suggests, usually seen near farm buildings, and its plu age is paler than that of other members of t family, sandy above and white underneat The tawny owl frequents woods and is mu darker in color, rich brown with light and da streaks. The short-eared owl has a distincti feature of its own: two tufts of head feathe These look like ears and have given the bird name, but they aren't ears at all. The ears the owl are openings on the side of the hea they are hidden by feathers.

On the left, one of the weirdest mammals: the bat. Below, the short-eared owl, hunting by night.

On a June night, more melodious notes min-gle with the strange noises of the owls and the soft whirr of the bats. Songs of birds like the nightingale ring out from the trees—but by August these summer visitors sense the near-ness of fall and have stopped singing.

Viper, or adder

Grass snake

Reptiles

Everything is still. It is so hot that the birds have stopped twittering and many other creatures are sleeping the afternoon away in the shade of a fern or a bush. But one group of animals is very happy with the heat: the reptiles. They are cold-blooded creatures whose bodies follow changes in external temperatures. They stay only just alive in the long winter months when the cold forces them underground, but they are quick and agile when it is hot. The biggest reptiles, the crocodiles, are found only in hot countries, in marshy areas.

Reptiles are vertebrates, one step higher in the scale than the amphibians, though the two groups are similar in many ways. Amphibians' eggs have no outer covering to protect them when they are exposed to air, so they have to be laid in water, and young amphibians start their lives in water, breathing by means of gills. Reptiles, on the other hand, lay their eggs on land and their young breathe through lungs as soon as they are born. Reptiles move mainly by crawling, since their four short legs are too weak to give proper support to their bodies. In some reptiles, the blindworm, for example, legs

never appear, but they are present in the skeleton. Most snakes do not even have them in skeletal form.

Making the most of the sunshine on a warm rock is a lizard. It is pressed flat against the rock with its four legs splayed out and only its head erect. Every now and then its sticky tongue flashes out to trap a fly. It is not too busy to notice that it is being watched, and it darts away quickly if anyone ventures too close. If an enemy should catch it by its tail, the tail will snap off to allow the lizard to escape. This is a normal defense mechanism and another tail will soon grow.

Reptiles, especially snakes, are not well-liked since many, like the rattlesnake and copperhead snake of North America, are poisonous. Some countries have few poisonous snakes. In Britain, for instance, only the viper, or adder, is dangerous. This snake is about 24 inches long, brown in color with a double row of dark horizontal streaks right down the body. The head is triangular in shape, narrowing to a point at the front, and marked with a black V shape. As the jaws of a viper close on its victim, they auto-

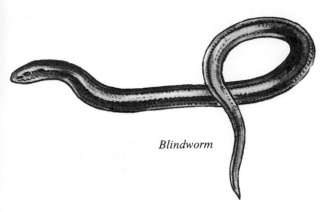

Blindworm

Reptiles often make people shudder since many are ugly or poisonous. Many reptiles, however, are harmless. In Britain, for instance, only the viper, or adder, is dangerous. On the right is the sticky-fingered gecko basking in the African sun; below is the timid lizard.

matically squeeze the poison gland and its fluid runs through the channels of the poison fang into the flesh of the victim.

The blindworm looks like a snake because its legs never develop, but it is actually a lizard. The rear part of its body is brittle, like many other lizards', and is just as easily replaced if it should break off during an attack by a predator. The blindworm is only about 16 inches long, black above and yellowish below; its body is covered with shiny scales.

Reptiles lay their eggs in carefully prepared spots. Snakes choose either a patch of ground that will be warmed by the sun or a steaming manure heap, so that their eggs will be kept warm. The eggs of the viper hatch inside the body of the female, producing young vipers about 2 inches long. Blindworms also give birth to live young.

In a very early period of prehistory, reptiles ruled the land. They were the first creatures to leave the water completely and adapt themselves fully to life on land. But today many people never come across a reptile in the wild; this is partly because reptiles are good at hiding.

When the tide goes out, it leaves piles of seaweed behind on the sand and rocks. Some farmers collect the seaweed to use as manure.

AUGUST

Life in the Sea

The sea is usually thought of as the kingdom of the fish, but it could equally well be called the kingdom of the plants, for there are meadows and forests in the sea just as there are on land. The Sargasso Sea, where eels go to spawn, is covered with floating plants as far as the eye can see. Sailors pick berries called Sargasso grapes there; they really do look like grapes, but they are actually just bladders full of air which keep the plants afloat. Like land plants, they are rich in chlorophyll.

These marine plants are called algae. Some have very broad, flat fronds; some are serrated, or notched on the side, and some are just thin threads like blades of grass. These blades can be up to 220 yards long. Certain types of blue algae dry up like hay when they are exposed to air and sunlight. They look dead, but as soon as the rising tide washes over them, they come back to life again and wave about with the movement of the water.

Algae are harvested because they are sometimes quite valuable. The long lines of seaweed that are washed up on the shore by the tide make an excellent fertilizer.

Perhaps the strangest marine creatures of all are found in crevices in the rocks. They haven't the suppleness, the grace or the speed of fish but they make up for these deficiencies by their very frightening weapons. Like the knights of the Middle Ages, they are protected by a suit of armor which covers their whole body. In some cases it is strong enough to break the teeth of any attacker. Their weapons are the spines on their backs and their razor-sharp pincers. These creatures can be as long as a man's forearm or smaller than his hand, but whatever their size, their appearance is frightening. Because their armor is rather like a crust, they are called crustaceans.

Crustaceans can be gathered from the rock pools left by the outgoing tide. There are crabs with five pairs of limbs. The first pair face forward and are armed with powerful pincers at the ends. Prawns and shrimps are caught with nets. Prawns are the bigger of the two, pinkish in color and with a long spear projecting from the head. The grayish-brown shrimp is smaller, but its head, too, is well armed with spines.

The biggest crustaceans, like the crawfish, can even sound quite terrifying. They flex their weapons with a menacing click.

The crawfish feeds on small fish, mollusks and algae. It is well provided with instruments to handle them: one pair of strong jaws (mandibles), two pairs of ancessory jaws (maxillae) and three pairs of foot jaws (called maxillipedes), which feel the food and carry it to the mouth.

Even though the crawfish is a marine animal and breathes by means of gills, it can stay alive out of water long enough to deal quite a vicious blow with its sharp tail to anyone who is foolish enough to pick it up.

The enormous pincers of the lobster and the long spines of the ugly spider crab are just as dangerous. Fortunately, most people only see them on the table, where their succulent flesh forms the base of many dishes prepared for special occasions.

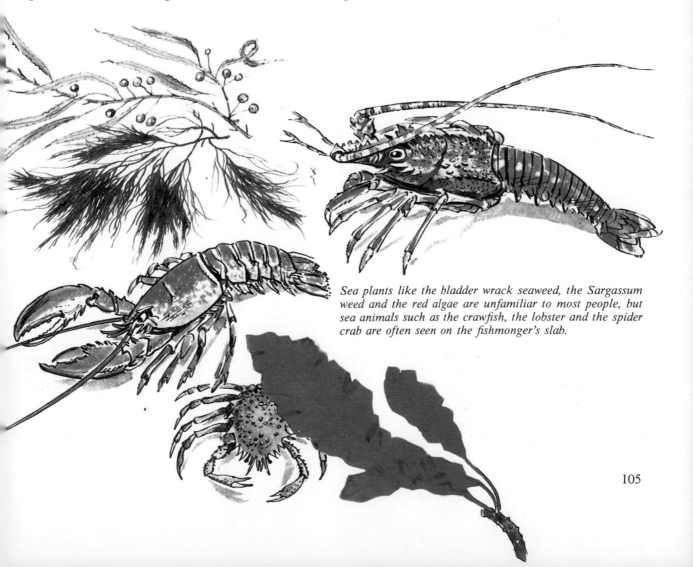

Sea plants like the bladder wrack seaweed, the Sargassum weed and the red algae are unfamiliar to most people, but sea animals such as the crawfish, the lobster and the spider crab are often seen on the fishmonger's slab.

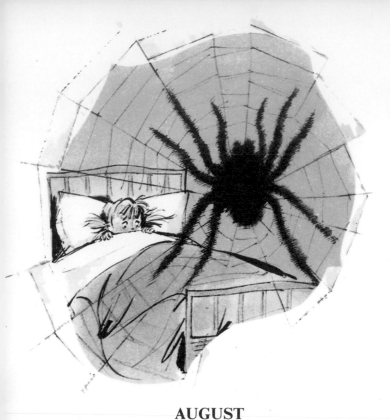

AUGUST

Spiders

Spiders are used as monsters by writers of science fiction, but though their appearance under a microscope is rather fearsome, they never reach the giant proportions described in such stories. Only a few kinds, such as the black widow spider of North America and the jockey spider of Australia, are dangerous to human beings.

Most small spiders reserve their poison for the creatures they prey on, for the spider is a carnivore. It likes to eat its food fresh, and it injects its poison into a victim only in order to paralyze it.

A spider may be loosely referred to as an insect, but this is not technically correct; the most obvious difference is that, whereas insects have six legs, the spider has eight. Also, an insect's body is clearly divided into three parts (head, thorax and abdomen), while in the spider's body it is impossible to tell where the head ends and the thorax begins. There are differences in organs, too. The spider has neither the antennae nor the compound faceted eyes of the insect, but it is well equipped with its six or eight simple eyes. The field spider or harvestman (commonly known as daddy long-legs because of its very long, hair-fine legs) is a member of the spider family but has only two eyes. Attached to a spider's body in front of the legs are two joined palpi, or foot jaws, which grope and feel. The legs themselves are provided with suction pads or claws and also tufts of hair which make them sensitive to the slightest movement on the web.

The most significant difference between the spider and most members of the insect group is that it does not undergo metamorphosis: when the young spiders emerge from their eggs, which the mother often carries in a silk cocoon under her abdomen, they are already adults in miniature. The mother spider cares for her eggs

The sheet web of the agalena spider

Field spider (daddy-long-legs)

Eggs of the argiope spider in their silky cocoon, or egg sac

and watches over her young with as much diligence as the more sophisticated mammals.

The web is perhaps the most interesting part of the spider's story. The delicate and complicated structure of the web can best be seen when the early morning sun falls on the dew-covered webs draped over the hedges. Not all spiders spin webs, and different types of spiders spin webs of different patterns, but the best-known one is the circular, or orb, web of the garden spider. A sticky liquid produced by glands in the spider's abdomen is passed through spinnerets at the tip of the abdomen. On contact with air, this liquid solidifies into a thread and the spider twists the threads from the spinnerets together to make a strong silken "cord." This it spins into a web, first making the frame and then filling it in, as in weaving. Once the trap is laid, the spider hides close by and watches. If a very large fly or wasp is entrapped, it can damage the web as it thrashes about trying to disentangle itself. The spider emerges and binds its wings and legs with more sticky thread until it is sufficiently disarmed for the spider to inflict its paralyzing bite. Since the spider depends on this precious silk for its food, it does not waste it.

The garden spider, Araneus diadematus. *On cool mornings when there is a heavy dew, the beautiful webs of these spiders sparkle all over the garden.*

SEPTEMBER

Berries for Jams

It is time to go blackberrying. Eager parties set out for the fields and lanes, armed with cans and waterproof bags. They are already musing about delicious jams to be made from the blackberry and other berries.

But they need to tread carefully. The blackberry bush, or bramble, does not give up its fruit easily. Its stems are covered with thorns and so are the undersides of the leaves. They clutch onto clothes and hair and are very painful to bare arms and legs. The thorns are not the only hazard; there are creeping stems, too. If you get your foot caught in a prickly stem and lift up the stem gingerly to free yourself

Familiar fruit: the blackberry which grows wild in hedgerows, the fragrant raspberry and the succulent strawberry.

108

you find you cannot do so because it is fastened at both ends. One end is attached to the main bush and the other has taken root in the ground a little way off. If you pull hard enough to dislodge the root, you disturb yet another stem growing from it and anchored in the ground still farther on. These creeping stems are called stolons.

This tangled growth quickly strangles other vegetation on any land that is not well tended. Because brambles are so dense and knotted and so forbidding to any trespasser, the farmer uses them as hedges, but he has to cut them back sharply to stop them invading his fields.

There are plenty of blackberries. This is no surprise after the masses of flowers that covered the bushes in spring. The flower of the blackberry is very like that of the wild rose, though smaller: it is pale pink, with five petals and five sepals. When the petals, sepals and stamens are stripped off the blackberry flower, all that is left is the stem, or peduncle, with its swollen tip, the receptacle. Clustered around the receptacle are some tiny green balls, the ovaries, each containing a seed. During the summer the blackberry flowers have lost their petals and the receptacles and ovaries have grown bigger. The ovaries have swollen up

around the seeds to protect them and provide nourishment. This cluster of swollen ovaries, dark and juicy, is the blackberry. When it is picked, it leaves the tasteless white receptacle behind on the peduncle.

The flowers of the strawberry and raspberry are very similar to those of the blackberry: they all belong to the family of the Rosaceae, but whereas the fruits of raspberry and blackberry are also similar, the strawberry is different. The sweet juicy flesh of the strawberry is not formed from the ovaries but from the receptacle, which has swollen to provide food and protection for the seeds. The seeds are easily seen, dotted on the shiny surface of the fruit. Because of its structure, a botanist would call the strawberry a false fruit, but this makes no difference to the flavor!

The strawberry plant does not depend on its seeds for reproduction. Its runners, or stolons, are much more reliable. They are shorter than those of the blackberry and have no thorns, but they serve the same purpose. The raspberry produces stolons, too. Stolons take root at some distance from the parent plant and the new roots remain linked to the parent by the stolons and feed from it until they are strong enough to break the link and thrive independently.

The Science of Flowers

Fall is approaching. There are fewer flowers around. Since the year began, flowers of all shapes and colors have bloomed in the woods, fields and gardens. There are so many different kinds that it seems impossible that anyone could distinguish them all, one from another—but the botanist can.

The botanist has no special secret. All he needs is a good pair of eyes and occasionally a magnifying glass. With this equipment, he has managed to sort out the world of plants. He lists the plants and classifies them in a special book called "Flora."

These are some of the main groups of plants:

Rosaceae

The flowers of this group have many stamens attached to the calyx. The flower itself is regular in shape, usually with four or five petals. In this family are the strawberry, raspberry, blackberry, plum, cherry, hawthorn and wild rose. The garden rose has more than five petals; it is a wild rose that has been altered by man.

Compositae

In this group, each flowerhead is actually composed of numerous small flowers. Members are the daisy, dandelion, sunflower, and marigold.

Papilionaceae

Each flower, with its five individually shaped petals, looks like a butterfly; the large central petal is known as the standard and below it come two wings and two keel petals. The fruit of this type of plant is a pod. Alfalfa and clover belong here, as do the pea and bean.

Solanaceae

These flowers have five petals joined together and five stamens. The flowers of the potato plant and the tomato belong to this family.

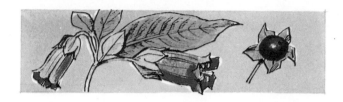

Gramineae

In this group come the wild grasses and the cereals, with their distinctive spike, or ear.

Cruciferae

These flowers have four petals and four sepals arranged in the form of a cross. The flowers usually grow in clusters, but if you look closely at each individual one, you will see that they all have six stamens, four long and two short. The wallflower, cabbage and radish are members.

Umbelliferae

These flowers look like open umbrellas. The tiny flowers are set on individual stems, which are short at the center and longer toward the edges. To this family belong the carrot, parsley, chervil, celery, and the poisonous hemlock.

Labiatae

The Latin word *labium*, meaning "lip," gives this group its name because the flower opens and shuts like a mouth if you squeeze it slightly. These plants are easy to recognize by their square stalk, and each one has a striking smell. They include mint, sage, balm and the white dead nettle, the one that does not sting.

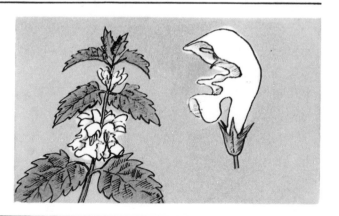

SEPTEMBER

Trees of the Forest

Nothing is duller than to walk through a forest with nothing to say about a tree except, "It's a tree!" It is not too difficult to be able to call every tree by its proper name and perhaps even to be able to say something about it.

Oak trees are sometimes called the kings of the forest. They provide the carpenter with his hardest and most resistant wood. The beams of palaces and old churches are made of oak because it grows harder as it ages. The oak leaf is easy to recognize: it is cut around the edges, not into sharp teeth but into gently rounded lobes. The fruit of the oak, the acorn, used to be relied on to feed pigs and was even used, in times of famine, to feed their masters as well. The bark of the oak, the tan, is used to process animal hide and turn it into leather.

Of all the trees in the forest, the sweet chestnuts are usually the oldest. Some are more than a thousand years old. Their wood is less solid than oak, but it is less open to attack by worms and less attractive to spiders, and these features make it ideal for high rafters in barns and for the naves in churches. It is a wood also liked by the cooper, a man who makes barrels, because it is tough yet pliable. The chestnut tree is easy to pick out in autumn when the chest-

The trees on the left, the fir, the spruce and the pine, are conifers, or cone bearers. Above right are a leaf and the winged seeds of the maple.

nuts burst out of their prickly cases and fall to the ground. The leaf of the chestnut is narrow, with serrated edges.

The wood of the beech tree is a favorite of the cabinetmaker; it is strong and of a close, even texture. The beech is difficult to distinguish from the hornbeam since both leaves are similar in shape and slightly scalloped around the edges. They can best be identified by their fruit. The fruit of the hornbeam is attached to a leafy bract whereas the beechnut is borne on a bare stem. The beechnut is rich in oil and for this reason is popular with the forest creatures.

The holly, the silver birch and the maple are all easy to identify. The holly's shiny leaves are green all the year around; they look attractive but their prickles are very sharp. The silvery bark of the birch gives the tree its name. Of all deciduous trees (those whose leaves fall in the autumn), the birch can best withstand the cold and so it is common in countries which suffer a long, hard winter. The sap of the silver birch yields a type of sugar from which a beverage is made in some countries. An even richer and

more plentiful product, maple syrup, is provided by the sap of the maple tree, both in the northeastern United States and in Canada. The maple's deeply veined leaf, the national emblem of Canada, has five distinct divisions and is very like that of the sycamore. Both have winged seeds. These twirl gracefully in the air as they fall from the tree.

Pines and firs are usually found deep in the forest. Pines are the trees with long green needles in clusters, and firs have flatter and shorter needles arranged singly.

The beech, the oak and the slender silver birch

AUTUMN

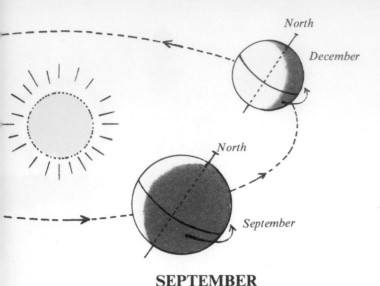

SEPTEMBER

Autumn Equinox

Since midsummer, when the night was the shortest of the year, the Earth has continued its course around the sun. It is now three quarters of the way along its annual journey and the nights are growing longer and longer.

Yesterday, the North Pole was still bathed in sunlight for the entire twenty-four hours of the day and the South Pole was still in total darkness. Today, the Earth has reached a point exactly in line with the sun's axis. At the two poles, and over all the Earth as well, day and night will be the same length of time; it is the autumn equinox, which marks the end of summer.

But, from tomorrow, the perpetual rotation of the Earth will plunge the North Pole into darkness and the South Pole will be flooded

It is difficult to show on paper the movement and the different positions of the Earth in relation to the sun. At the time of the equinox, the light of the sun falls straight along the axis of the poles, just as if the axis were upright. So the whole Earth has a 12-hour day and a 12-hour night (left).

with light. And it will remain like this for six months, until the spring equinox brings daylight to the North Pole again.

In the Northern Hemisphere the sun no longer climbs so high above the horizon, and the weather is growing colder.

In fall, as in spring, the tilt of the Earth throws the climate into confusion. The fine bright days of summer are gone and August storms are followed by winter rain. The wind blows in angry gusts, bending the trees and shaking their branches; the first leaves of autumn fall to the ground and wasps and dormice feast on fallen fruit. There is the smell of smoke drifting over the bare fields as the farmers burn the potato tops now that the crop is in. In the meadows they are busy mowing for the second time in the year, to bring in the aftergrass that grows after the first hay crop has been harvested.

But the autumn equinox makes its biggest impact by the sea, often in a tragic way. All the land is being buffeted by the stormy fall weather, but along the coasts there is the additional problem of extra-high tides. Then the sea may attack dikes, crash over breakwaters and harbor walls, and hurl itself up the estuaries against the flow of the river in a terrifying wall of water, a tidal bore.

When the force of the wind is added to the effect of the full tide, the sea invades the land, flooding fields, breaching dikes and devastating exposed villages. This is exactly what happens in fall when the wind is blowing from the sea, which is cold, toward the land, which has been warmed by the summer sun. The wind blows in the same direction as the incoming tide, supporting it and doubling its effect. (In the spring, it was the other way around: the wind was blowing from the land, which was cold after the winter, toward the warmer sea. Then the wind was acting against the tide, protecting the coasts from the invasion of the water.) This is why storms at the time of the autumn equinox are feared much more than those in the spring. When the reduction in air pressure which always accompanies a storm allows the tide to rise higher than usual, and when this is combined with the "pull" of the moon and the violent wind, the result is not just a high tide battering the coast, but a devastating tidal bore.

Seven hundred years ago, Holland had a straight, flat coastline, with quiet little villages rising behind it. In the course of one terrible onslaught by the tide, the coast caved in and eighty villages and their inhabitants were engulfed. The sea reshaped the coastline, forming that inland pocket of water called the Zuider Zee. At present, work is going on to fill in this pocket. By gigantic engineering projects, the Dutch people are struggling to repair, seven hundred years after the event, the damage inflicted in a few hours by a raging sea.

The autumn equinox is often marked by violent storms. In Holland, they are now reclaiming all the land which was lost in a disaster of long ago. Below is the immensely strong dike which will protect the land reclaimed from the Zuider Zee (right).

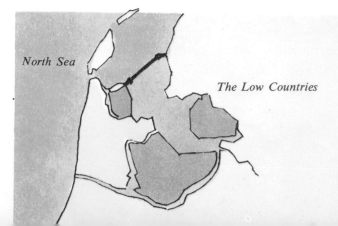

North Sea

The Low Countries

OCTOBER

The Grape Harvest

In America the word "harvest" usually means gathering in the wheat, corn, or other grains, although other crops—cotton, hay, tobacco, potatoes, grapes—are also important. But for people in France, the world's greatest wine-producing country, the harvest above all others is that of the grapes.

The harvest takes place in October. The vineyards are full of busy people. Laughter and singing ring out across the vine-covered slopes. It shows the relief that everyone concerned with the vineyard feels because the time has come to gather the grapes and no last-minute crisis has affected the crop.

Problems arise as soon as work in the vineyard begins in early January, when the ground between the rows of vine stocks is prepared. Before the spring comes, the vines have to be pruned, and it is a specialist's job to trim them in such a way that they will produce plenty of good-quality fruit. Each bud produces a branch, and each branch has to be trained into a position where it will get most benefit from the air and sun and where it can be easily reached by the vineyard workers. April, when the vine flowers, is a particularly anxious time; if the overnight temperature falls unusually low and there is a frost, the flowers may wither before they are fertilized and there will be no fruit. In an emergency, artificial fog is sometimes used to prevent frost falling on the vines. Once the bunches of grapes form, it is a struggle to protect them while they are developing

and ripening; they can be severely damaged by rust, mildew and many different insects. The vines must be sprayed time and again during this period.

By October the long days of summer sun have ripened the grapes. Each additional sunny day makes them a little sweeter. They must be left on the vine until the last possible moment so that they are picked at their best, and yet there is the constant risk of the whole crop being ruined in a few moments by a sudden shower of hail or an unexpected storm.

Now all worries are behind them as the grape-pickers work away with their shears, clipping off the bunches and laying them in baskets. From the baskets they are loaded into crates to be taken to a waiting cart, which then carries them off to the enormous vats waiting in the winegrower's cellars.

In a way, a grape is like an egg; the only essential difference is that the grape contains the germ of a plant while the egg contains the germ of an animal. The egg has a shell and the grape has a tough skin which protects it from damage by rough weather and insect bites. The "white" of the grape is the translucent pulp that makes such a delicious dessert and its "yolk" is the pip enclosed in a fine skin. All eggs and fruits are made up of the same three indispensable parts: first, an outer coat (in the form of a leathery skin or a prickly case or a shell) as a protection against buffeting by the weather, damp and extreme heat or cold; second, as further cushioning and as a reserve food supply, the nutritious flesh or pulp; third, usually in the very center, the precious germ or seed of some future living thing—whether it be an oak tree, a bean, a chicken, or a grape.

Below the bunch of grapes on the right is one grape cut in half, and beside it is one of its pips, which contains the germ of the future vine.

OCTOBER

Wine

The grapes are safely gathered in, but there is no time to sit back and relax. If they are not processed immediately, they may lose quality and all the effort of producing them would be wasted. The table grapes have already been sent into town to be marketed. Now the grapes for wine need attention.

In the winegrower's cellars everything is ready. The enormous vat has been cleaned, the screw on the winepress has been oiled and the casks have been disinfected with sulphur fumes and bound with new hoops. Sometimes the pressing of the grapes starts out in the vineyard as soon as they are picked off the vine, but the work begins in earnest when they reach the cellars. They are piled into enormous vats and pressed. Machines are used for pressing nowadays but at one time the juice was squeezed out of the grapes by people dancing on them with their bare feet. This was called "treading the grapes" and was part of a grand celebration traditional at harvest time.

As the press is tightened, the juice pours out from the bottom of the vat; although not yet fit to be called wine, it is powerful enough to make anyone drunk. Once the juice has been squeezed out, it begins to "work," or ferment. This juice, from black grapes, can become either white or red wine. For white wine, the juice alone is used. For red wine, the juice is fermented together with the mush of grape skins, stalks and pips.

The mixture in the fermenting vats seethes and bubbles. Little organisms from the grape skins are now at work in the juice, carrying out chemical changes. The most important of these changes, from the winegrower's point of view, is the transformation of sugar into alcohol. The more sugar there is in the juice the more alcohol will be produced during fermentation, and the better the wine will be. This explains why the winegrower waited until the last possible moment to start picking the grapes: each extra day of sun could produce more sugar in the grapes and improve the quality of his wine.

The bubbling mess in the vat is like thick mud. There is a lot still to be done before it becomes the clear red wine that glows like a ruby in the glass. When the juice has finished fermenting in the vat, it is drawn off and poured, or decanted, several times into casks. Each time it is filtered and purified.

Many months after the harvest, it is at last bottled. Even at this stage it is still "young"; it would not be mellow enough to please the pa-

...nce is famous all over the world for its wines. The bot-... above represent only a few of the main wine-producing ...as. Above left, facing page: a winepress in action, with ... grape juice pouring out of the vat, and a worker in-...cting the contents of the fermenting vat. Above right: ...inegrower sampling some red wine drawn from a cask. ...n after bottling, it will continue to be stored and sam-...d regularly until judged mature enough for drinking.

... of a connoisseur. It is left to mature in ...lts cut into the hillside, where the tempera-...e and the degree of humidity are carefully ...ntrolled. The wine is still alive, still develop-..., in the bottles. At last, after regular sam-...ng, the winegrower pronounces it ready for

drinking. He gives each bottle its special label. The label indicated the region or origin of the wine (Burgundy, Bordeaux, Alsace, Anjou) and also, in the case of very high quality wine, the name of the particular vineyard that produced it: Meursault, Vouvray, Clos-Vougeot, Chateau-Lafite and many others. One more important detail is inscribed on the label: the date—that is, the year when the grapes were harvested. Some years are renowned for wine, because they had long hot summers to sweeten the grapes and so produced a wine of unusually high quality.

OCTOBER

Oil from Plants

In nature, everything makes the most of the summer while it lasts and finds some way of making provision for the barren winter. Man has laid in stocks of grain, potatoes, fruit and so on for himself, and fodder for his animals, to see them both through to the following summer. In the case of wine, however, he is storing a product that will keep much longer than one winter, and the same is true of another agricultural product: oil. It is well known that plants provide flour, sugar and wine; they also provide fat, a most important item in the human diet, in the form of oil. Demand for this oil has greatly increased, since fat extracted from plants is becoming more popular for cooking than animal fats that were once in general use.

Walnuts are a source of oil. They are grown in many places, including the United States,

Europe and China, and October is the usual month to pick them. While the nuts are still green, the trees are tapped with long wooden poles to shake down the nuts. It is the edible kernel of the nut that is rich in oil, and reaching it, even when the nut has been brought down, is like hunting for hidden treasure. First you have to remove the thick green outer husk and crack the hard wooden shell. The paper partitions inside have to be pulled apart and the white kernel is at last revealed beneath its wrinkled brown skin. It is easy to demonstrate how rich in oil this kernel is; if you rub it on a piece of paper, it leaves a permanent stain and makes the paper almost transparent. It is even possible to make a very simple oil lamp by fixing a cotton wick into a walnut shell.

The olive yields more oil than the walnut and needs a warmer climate. It thrives in

Many different plants yield oil. In Sicily (facing page) long wooden poles are being used to harvest olives. Walnuts are picked by the same method.

South of France and especially in Spain, Italy and Greece. Groundnuts (peanuts) need a tropical climate. Their name indicates an unusual feature of their development: like potatoes, they grow and ripen underground. The coconut provides an even more abundant supply of oil; it grows on coconut palms in tropical islands of the Pacific Ocean. Whatever the source of oil, whether it is to be drawn from walnuts, olives, groundnuts or coconuts, or from seeds rich in oil like poppy seed, sunflower seed or linseed, the big problem is how to extract the largest possible quantity of the pure, clear oil that housewives want to buy.

The principle behind the operation is simple: the liquid is extracted from the nut or seed by crushing it. The sap that flows during the first pressing is the virgin oil, the purest and most expensive. After the first pressing, the remains of the nut or seed are tied tightly into sacks and pressed a second time either by hand or

Groundnuts (peanuts) are shown below on their underground stems. The picture on the right shows coconut palms, a coconut with half its fibrous outer husk removed and, beside it, a piece of broken shell showing the edible white center of the nut.

machine. In large concerns, the nuts are crushed by hydraulic presses. The oil extracted during the second pressing is of inferior quality. The greasy mess then left in the sacks still contains some oil; after hot water is added to help it flow, a last pressing is made and the cheapest oil, for industrial use, is extracted.

Nothing is wasted. Slabs of debris are left in the flattened sacks and these are still rich in fat. They are sold to farmers as cattle cake.

OCTOBER

Sugar

Wine and oil—these are two products that the work of man has won from the rich earth in October. But that is only part of the story. In October he also harvests the plants that produce sugar.

Years ago, the only sweet food available in many countries was honey from the bee. It was a rare delicacy and very expensive. Today bee-keepers are still busy cultivating bees to rob them of their treasure. The bees work hard all summer to collect a store of honey which will keep the hive going throughout the winter; the store it in honeycombs which they make out o wax. By autumn the hive is well stocked, so th beekeeper chooses this time of year to take away the honeycombs. He replaces the honey combs with artificial frames filled with impur sugar (molasses) which will keep the bees aliv through the winter but enable him to profit fron their work. He dare not risk removing th honeycombs from the hive without taking specia precautions to protect himself against stings; h uses smoke to make the bees drowsy and h protects his face and hands with a mask an gloves.

Honey, used mostly as a spread, is still one c our most delightful foods. But to supply his eno mous needs for a substance to sweeten food man now depends chiefly on two plants—th sugar cane and the sugar beet. The sugar can grows in hot, wet climates in countries such a

In the West Indies, sugar cane is an important crop. Th inset picture below left shows the resemblance of a piece sugar cane to bamboo. The cane is tasty to chew becau. it is full of sweet pith.

the West Indies, Brazil, India and the Philippines. The stems are about six yards tall and about two inches across; they are full of soft pith which contains sweet sap.

Sugar beet thrives in heavy soil and in mild climates. It is produced in large quantities in Europe, as well as North America. This plant has large leaves and stores food, in the form of sugar, in its fat creamy-colored root.

Sugar beet has to be brought in before the frosts start. The plants are uprooted and the leaves are chopped off and left lying in the fields. It is the roots that are needed, and these are loaded onto carts which take them to the refinery; this is a strange factory which often stands isolated in open country and is in action only a few months each year. Simply to extract a sweet substance from the sugar beet does not require much effort. The root is cut into thin slices and simmered in water. Then the liquid is strained off and heated gently to allow the water to evaporate. It leaves behind in the saucepan a dark treacly liquid, very like the molasses that the beekeeper used to replace the honey in the hive.

But this dark liquid would not satisfy today's housewife. She wants crisp white cubes of sugar that dissolve easily or shining white crystals of granulated sugar. So the processing of the sugar beet in the refinery is rather more complicated than the saucepan method. Steam is used to force the sweet syrup out of the roots and the refined white sugar is obtained after a series of cleaning, filtering and purifying processes. The remains of the plant become cattle food. The refining of sugar from cane is much the same as for sugar beet except that it is the stems that are crushed to extract the sweet syrup. The sugar from the cane is not quite so white as that from sugar beet but is more nutritious.

Sugar is one of the many substances that contain carbon; you could call it sunlight in solid form. It is a vital source of energy for the body, which is especially needed as the cold winter days approach.

Sugar beet thrives in the mild areas of Europe and North America. When raw, it doesn't taste as good as sugar cane. The sweet juice from both plants has to be processed and refined to make it into the pure white sugar we know.

OCTOBER

Textiles

A weaver's shuttle

Nature is the source of food and drink and medicines. It is also the source of many of the materials that protect the body from extremes of heat or cold; these materials come from both animals and plants.

Sheep are shorn in summer. They seem glad to be rid of their heavy fleece, but the sheep shearers are not working only for the comfort of the sheep; the fleece is valuable wool. When wool is first shorn from the sheep, it is dirty, greasy and foul-smelling. It goes to the mills where it has to be cleaned, spun, combed, dyed and woven before it is ready for the tailor's workroom or the fabric department of a big store.

To manufacture soft, lightweight woolen material of all colors from the dirty, matted fleece of the sheep is quite an achievement, but the story of silk manufacture is an even greater tribute to man's ingenuity. This shiny, luxurious fabric comes from a caterpillar, the silkworm, which is the larva of an unattractive, colorless moth. This moth is an insect, which means that it undergoes the usual metamorphosis from egg to larva to pupa and finally to moth. When it is ready to enter the pupal stage, the larva of the silkworm produces a fine thread which it winds around and around itself to form a protective cocoon. The cocoon is made of a single long thread (more than a thousand yards long) which is very strong. The silk manufacturer must take this thread before the larva emerges from the cocoon and destroys it. The cocoon is plunged into boiling water to kill the sleeping larva, and then the long thread is unwound. It is so fine it has to be spun with other threads to be suitable for weaving into satins, silk crepes and velvets.

Spiders also spin silk cocoons to carry their eggs in, but so far manufacturers have had no success in making thread or material from the spider's silk.

Cotton and linen come from plants. Cotton is manufactured from the downy covering of the seeds of the cotton plant, which grows mainly in the United States and in Egypt. Linen comes from flax which grows in Europe. Irish linen is famous. Flax grows to a height of almost twenty inches and the fields full of waving blue flowers are a pretty sight. The plants are cut when the seeds have formed and are left tied up in bundles to dry out in the fields. They are then threshed to beat out the seeds which yield oil (linseed oil). The fibrous stems that remain are soaked in running water for a fortnight to clean and soften them. The long supple threads of linen then separate easily from the woody fibers. A final combing removes any impurities and the threads are then ready to be spun and woven into fine quality linen or stronger fabrics like canvas. Even though the woody fibers cannot be used for spinning and weaving, they are not thrown out, and sailors have good reason to be glad of them. They are known as "tow" and are used for filling and sealing cracks and joints in wooden boats.

These are just a few of the animals and plants that provide the textiles for our comfort and well-being.

The blue flowers of the flax and bundles of flax drying in the fields

The cotton plant and cotton-harvesting in the United States

The silkworm: moth laying eggs, larva eating a mulberry leaf, the start of the pupal stage and the finished cocoon.

Fungi

The plants called fungi have no trunk, no branches, no leaves, no flowers and no true roots. They do not even have chlorophyll which means that they are quite different from any plants mentioned so far because they cannot make their own food by photosynthesis. They grow in damp earth, on a rotting tree trunk, in leaf mold or even on decaying animal matter. The fungi that feed on these different types of decomposing material are called saprophytes. Some fungi live off organisms that are still alive and these are called parasites.

Autumn is the best season to watch out for these fungi. They are usually easy to find because they are brightly colored. They come in all shades except the usual dark green of a plant, so they stand out against the grass and the dark tree trunks in the woods.

Fungi sometimes reproduce by sending up toadstools. Once the toadstools are mature they shower the ground with a fine powder which falls from the gills beneath their caps. This powder consists of millions of cells called spores. If the spores fall into suitable ground they will begin to grow. They develop from single cells into chains of cells and eventually form a whole network capable of producing its own toadstools. The spores are difficult to see

There are fungi growing everywhere in the fields and woods, perhaps on an old tree stump like the polyporus type above. On the left is a poisonous toadstool, the death cup (Amarita phalloides). As it develops, the young toadstool bursts through a membrane which enclosed it completely at first. This is the volva, and the remnants of it cling to the adult toadstool, leaving a ring round the upper part of the stalk and a pouch at the base.

128

when the toadstool is in its natural position, but if you lay the cap of a toadstool on a sheet of paper, some of the powder will fall and will show up clearly on the paper. There is no need to do this with all toadstools; you only need to brush against some types, such as puffballs, and clouds of spores will shoot into the air.

Though many fungi are safe and delicious to eat, many are harmful. As a matter of fact, poisonous species often resemble, or are closely related to, edible species. And some of the

membrane which once enclosed the young toadstool completely)

2. A white ring round the stalk

3. White gills on the underside of the cap

The edible field mushroom and the larger horse mushroom grow wild in the fields. The gills are pale pink at first and then gradually turn black. Other edible fungi include the cep *(Boletus edulis),* which has a large brown cap, and spongy flesh full of little holes.

One of the deadliest fungi is the death cup

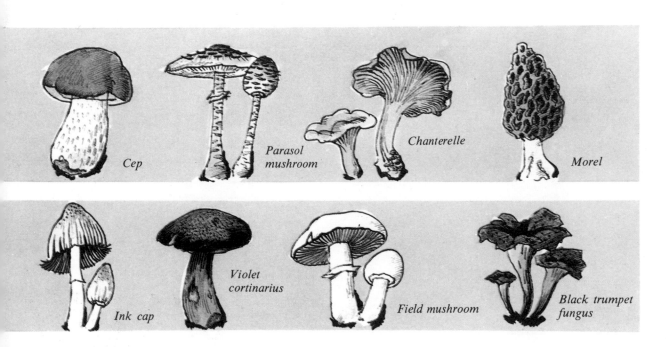

Cep

Parasol mushroom

Chanterelle

Morel

Ink cap

Violet cortinarius

Field mushroom

Black trumpet fungus

poisonous ones are so deadly that doctors have no reliable antidote for them! That is why you should never pick *any* wild mushrooms or toadstools to eat.

Even without knowing all the various names of fungi, it is possible to recognize some of the features that poisonous fungi have in common. A toadstool which has the following features must *never* be eaten:

1. A volva, which is a sort of pouch around the base of the stalk (it is the remains of a

(Amanita phalloides). It is especially dangerous because it is very common and because it can easily be mistaken for a field mushroom. It grows in woods, has a greenish cap, white gills and a volva at the base of the stalk.

Looking for toadstools in the fields and woods can be great fun, but because of the danger, remember that you must never take even the tiniest taste of any fungi that has not been positively identified as safe by someone who really is an expert.

Cranes

OCTOBER

Departures

In October, as winter approaches, the last of the migrant birds prepare to leave for warmer climates.

The swallows do not leave as quietly as they came. A lot of preparations are necessary before they can set out on their long flight over mountain and sea. The young birds that were hatched in the spring and have never made the journey before have to be strong enough for the flight. The young of swallows summering in Europe are never hatched in Asia or Africa but always in their European habitats in nests that have probably been occupied by the same family for many years.

For a long time before their departure, swallows gather together regularly on telegraph wires and twitter incessantly as if they were making plans; they practice flying in groups and taking off and returning together, just as if they were pilots on a training session. Then one day they fly off for good, leaving their homes

The map on the right shows the different parts of Africa where swallows from Europe spend the winter. They travel across mountain and sea, and their journey is full of dangers, yet in spring they will face them all again on the return journey.

and favorite perches behind until next spring. The dangers of the journey are so great that some will not survive to return.

The bigger birds leave, too. From Europe the storks head for the south in ones and twos. Cranes from many northern regions fly overhead in their usual V formation. At their head is the strongest and most experienced bird, battling its way through the wind and pointing the

Wild geese migrate southward to temperate zones in autumn; they fly in a V formation.

ay. The others fall in behind, the tips of their ings almost touching. They fly as a team, ther like racing cyclists or runners, helping ie another along and changing places to give ed teammates an easier position. Some wild icks are also on the move; the shy teal, for ample, may take its young from western irope as far as Egypt, and some even reach e Pacific Ocean and China.

Wild geese are traveling, too, but not to the me destinations. These birds are among those at migrate from northern zones in autumn to end the winter in temperate areas. They are very cautious and land only in wide open spaces. They post sentries round their camp and the whole flock takes to the air at the slightest alarm.

All these migrant birds find their way by instinct. Without any compass, they fly as confidently as any pilot with his radar and his array of complicated dials. This instinct is most remarkable in the carrier pigeon. Whatever the season or however far away the pigeon is, it makes a beeline for home as soon as it has found its bearings, and it returns in the shortest possible time.

NOVEMBER

Seeking Shelter

The days are shortening. The air becomes colder. The outdoors, lately vociferous with the twitter of birds and the buzz of insects, falls silent.

This is the time, too, when trees and bushes shed the rich raiment of summer and autumn. In winter there will be too little sunshine for the leaves to be able to continue with photosynthesis. There is no longer any fruit on the trees needing to be nourished: it has ripened and fallen. So there is no work for the sap to do. It almost stops flowing through the trees and the leaves wither and fall to the ground. The will decompose and form humus, the natura manure that will enrich the soil, so that it ready to feed next year's plants.

The fruits—acorns, beechnuts and haze nuts—have fallen among the leaves, where the are sheltered from the worst of the gales. The will gradually absorb moisture to prepare fc

The leaves fall from deciduous trees; above is a sycamor and below is a pile of leaves, mainly oak, sheltering a acorn. Only the evergreens keep their leaves.

he return of milder days when they will start
o grow shoots.

Many animals flee from the winter cold, just
is the birds have done, but they cannot migrate
n search of the sun; instead they take refuge in
he earth. The blindworm, snake and lizard do
iot slide over the stones anymore; they are
urled up underground, asleep. The toads, too,
iave dug themselves well into the ground.

There are no butterflies flitting through the
;arden or bees hunting for nectar. The june bug
; now a horny chrysalis or a sleepy white

nimals retreat into the ground at the approach of winter.
he turtle (above right), the hedgehog (above), and the
ole (below right) burrow under the soil to hibernate.

orm buried in the soil. Flies are perhaps
eeping under logs or in the house under dusty
ld floorboards; we can't be sure, for exactly
here flies go in winter remains a mystery.

In the summer you can track the movements
f the mole by following his little hills of loose
iil across a field, but now he shows no sign of
fe. The dormouse has laid in a store of nuts,
i case he should be wide awake enough on a
inny winter day to need a snack, and has
iuggled down in an underground nest of grass
id leaves and bits of fluff.

Below ground, too, are the hedgehog and the
badger. At any other time of the year, they
would have been very interested to learn that
the slug was a near neighbor of theirs, but now
they do not care. The snail has drawn its eyes
into its head and its head into its shell and
sealed its shell off across the base with a water-
tight cover.

Plants and animals are sheltering in the
earth. Man too puts some of his precious food
stocks in the earth for safekeeping. He lays root
vegetables, potatoes and some types of animal
fodder in trenches in the ground and covers
them with layers of straw and soil to protect
them. These storage places are called silos.

NOVEMBER

The Life of a Tree

Now that the trees' main period of growth is finished for the year, the woodcutter returns to the forest. He has a lot of work to get through before spring, so he brings along a trailer as his headquarters. He uses it to store equipment in, as a shelter from heavy showers and as a place to prepare his lunch. When it gets dark, he locks it up for the night and goes off to the village in his truck.

The woodcutter's work is carefully planned for him by the forester. The trees that are to be cut down are especially marked. Only trees of the right age are felled, perhaps when twenty-five or thirty years old, and their location as well as their age must be taken into account. At one time, the felling of trees was completely haphazard and the results were disastrous in many mountain areas. When heavy rain fell,

water gushed down the mountainside. There were no trees left to break the force of the flow and no roots to hold the soil in place, so the flood water carried away the topsoil and the crops and even houses and roads. Now it is understood that a tree is a valuable reservoir of water. It stores and it regulates the flow of water through the earth. In fact, forests have a considerable effect on the size and the course of rivers.

There is a lot to be learned from the trunk of a tree that has just been felled. If you look at a cross section of the trunk, you will see that it consists of three quite different parts. The center is dark in color and solid; this is the heart wood. The paler, softer area of wood encircling the dark center is the sapwood, or alburnum, which is of relatively recent formation. The circumference of the circle is made up of the bark, which breaks off easily, and, just inside it, a moist layer called the liber, or inner bark. The liber is moist because the sap circulates through this part of the trunk. Moving up the vessels of the liber is crude sap carrying dissolved minerals from the soil up to the leaves and moving down other vessels is sap that has been enriched with material made by the leaves. Material made by photosynthesis is dis-

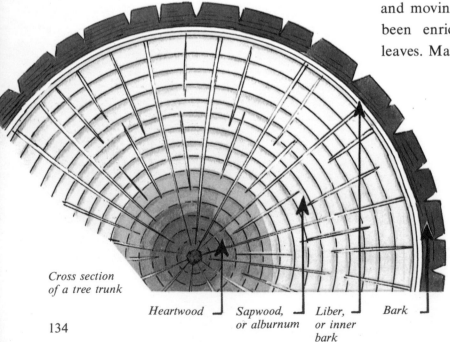

Cross section of a tree trunk

Heartwood ⌐ Sapwood, ⌐ Liber, ⌐ Bark ⌐
　　　　　or alburnum　or inner
　　　　　　　　　　　　bark

Bark of the oak tree

134

tributed to all parts of the tree by the sap. It is from this that wood is formed.

Because the sap does not circulate much in winter, no wood is formed at this time. Next spring a new layer of liber will develop under new bark to set the sap flowing around the tree and wood will be made again. Each time the sap stops circulating at the end of the summer, a dark ring forms around the trunk, and these circles, which appear reliably at the rate of one every year, indicate the age of the tree. It is by this method of counting rings in the trunk that it has been possible to determine the age of the giant redwood trees in California.

Trees that are three or four hundred years old and still standing are dead in the center. The only living part is the outer rim next to the bark. The material distributed by the sap feeds only the liber. That is why old trees are sometimes completely hollow; the heartwood has rotted or been gnawed away by animals and there is no way of replacing it. These trees are still alive, but they are unstable.

The blood of a vertebrate circulates through the entire organism. The "blood" of a plant, the sap, circulates only through the liber. This is one of the characteristics that distinguish the largest plants from the largest animals.

*A marten
in a hollow tree*

The finest giant redwood trees are in California. This giant conifer reaches a height of 300 feet and the trunk at its base has a diameter of between 30 and 50 feet. Some of these trees are more than 3,000 years old, so they were growing when Julius Caesar ruled in Rome (1), when the Crusaders set off for the East (2), or when Christopher Columbus discovered America (3).

135

Hunting

The countryside is not a very inviting place in November, but it is not deserted. In addition to the woodcutter and the occasional rambler, there are people out hunting.

A hunting party can mean anything from a couple of farmers out keeping pests in check or just enjoying a day's shooting to a full-scale hunt with horsemen in pink coats and baying hounds.

The farmers are probably out with their guns and a dog to hunt partridges or hares or rabbits. All through the summer the partridges have been watched over by the gamekeeper. Suddenly, on a given date in autumn, they find themselves at the mercy of the gun.

There is some reason for pursuing hares or rabbits; they could quickly overrun the countryside. Hares have four litters every year, with about three or four leverets in each litter. The farmers' fields of turnips, cabbages and clover

The colors of the young partridges blend in with the ploughed field and often protect them as they crouch in the furrows. The hare makes his home in a hollow in a field or glade, but he has powerful legs and ears to help him escape from hunters.

would soon suffer from the ravages of their sharp teeth if they were allowed to multiply at this rate.

Even more prolific are wild rabbits, which produce six or seven litters per year with about eight young rabbits in each. That means that, by autumn, one pair of rabbits have given birth to about fifty young ones, a rate of growth which obviously has to be checked. Rabbits live in burrows, not in the shallow hole in a clearing or ploughed field which the hare prefers, so it is possible to trap them without a chase. This is done by placing sacks over all the entrances to the burrow except one and then sending a ferret in. This savage little carnivore makes the rabbit panic and it is either caught by the ferret or driven out into one of the waiting sacks.

A conventional hunting party usually sets out in pursuit of a fox. The fox makes itself unpopular by attacks on chickens, especially as it causes far more damage than is necessary to satisfy its appetite. However, many people think that fox hunting is neither the most humane nor the most effective way of dealing

The wild boar, or pig, with female and young in its muddy lair. Such a family can devastate an entire field overnight when they set to work with their snouts and sharp tusks.

with this troublemaker. Although the fox is a
...iller, it has many good features: it is attractive
...n appearance with its reddish-brown coat and
...hick brush, it is intelligent in escaping from
...ursuers and it is a very hardworking and de-
...oted parent.

Partridges, rabbits and hares are inoffensive
...uarry, both for the hunter and his dogs. A
...ore dangerous occupation is hunting the wild
...oar, or pig, found in continental Europe and
...n parts of Asia and Africa. This animal can be
...hree feet long and two feet high, and the hunter
...as to be constantly on the alert against attack

by its two sharp tusks, with a weight of several
hundred pounds behind them. During the day
the boar family—two adults and as many as
ten young ones—lie low in their muddy lair in
the forest; at night they set out for the fields
that border the forest to hunt for food. They
root out and devour whatever crops they come
across and can devastate a whole field in one
night. The farmers have no alternative but to
defend their land against such attacks.

137

The wild rabbit (above) is snug in its burrow, well away from wind and rain. It will wait for better weather before venturing out. The ants are asleep in their anthill (right). The roof has been strengthened with soil and twigs.

NOVEMBER

At Home

It feels pleasant and secure to be warm and dry indoors when the wind is roaring outside and cold, driving rain is battering against the windowpanes.

Animals must feel the same way that we do, for whenever winter storms are raging, they, too, retreat into their homes. High up in the mountains the bear seeks out a cleft in the rocks or a hole in an old tree. It sleeps curled up like a huge dog, oblivious to the cold in its thick fur coat. Many other mammals seek shel-

ter from bad weather. The rabbit crouches on its bed of dry grass deep in its burrow and waits patiently, perhaps for as long as a week or more, for the weather to calm down before venturing out again.

Creatures that live in organized cities, like the ants and the bees, don't suffer much from the winter because their routine includes preparations to protect them against it.

There is practically no activity in the anthill now. The roof has been reinforced in good

138

time with a sort of cement mixture made of soil, straw, dead leaves and twigs. The queen has stopped laying eggs and is resting. The last batch of eggs hatched out at the end of October, so the work of feeding and rearing the larvae is finished.

Now the ants can live peacefully, completely enclosed in their anthill and feeding off the huge reserves of food which they gathered during the summer.

The inhabitants of the beehive might not fare so well after being robbed of their stocks of honey, but fortunately the beekeeper has substituted sweet syrup. This will be enough for them to be able to survive indoors until spring comes.

The substitute honeycombs are arranged around the outer walls to keep out the cold, and the whole community huddles around the queen in the center of the hive. The worker bees' only duty is fetching food, and that is an indoor job; they have sealed off the exit from the hive with a special sticky substance (propolis) to keep the cold wind out.

There are no male drones left in the hive. Their only function in the summer was to fertilize the queen's eggs, so in winter, when it is important not to have surplus mouths to feed, the workers kill the drones or chase them away before they close the hive.

Many birds leave before the November gales tear through the trees. Those that stay crouch low in some sort of shelter. Some die in the harsh winter when the storms are relentless and the food scarce, but many live to see the return of spring. The crossbill is lucky, for in November the new fir cones are opening and he can peck the seeds out of the cones with his sharp little bill.

A male crossbill pecks seeds from fir cones.

Medicinal Plants

From spring through autumn, man has carefully gathered all that nature has provided. He gathers not only the produce that makes up the main part of his diet but he collects also the roots, leaves or flowers from particular plants to use as health aids. His selection is based on many thousands of years of observation and experience.

Ever since man first inhabited the earth, he has tried to make use of everything that nature offered to fight disease and prolong his life. The knowledge he has gained has taught him to value the medicinal plants, the herbs,

very highly. They are still gathered every year and used a great deal despite the progress made in the fields of chemistry and medicine

Some people drink water in which the fragrant flowers of the lime tree or the scented leaves of the vervain have been soaked. These drinks are called infusions, and they are thought to help people sleep. Mint leaves are valued for their refreshing properties; camomile tea brewed from the camomile's bitter flowers, is sometimes used to soothe a stomachache.

It would take a book as thick as a dictionary to list all the virtues of herbs. There are people

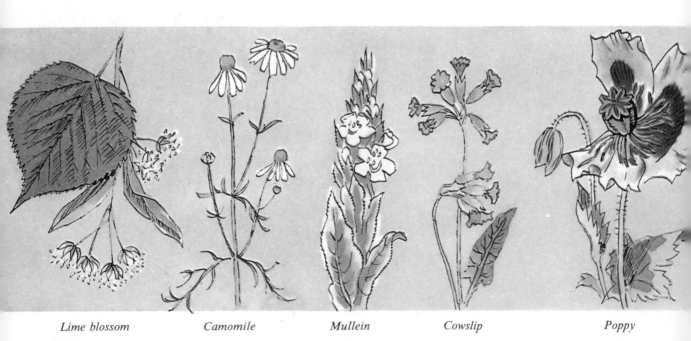

Lime blossom   *Camomile*   *Mullein*   *Cowslip*   *Poppy*

who recognize their medicinal effects by giving them very picturesque names: "sneezing herb," "lung herb," "wart herb," "doctors' wisdom" or "body health."

Some plants are thought to help the kidneys in purifying the blood by cleansing it of body waste. Among these are the dandelion, the cherry (the stalks are used), and the pansy.

To relieve a cough, cowslip or mullein are used. Lettuce has a tranquilizing effect or, if something more drastic is needed, a doctor may make very cautious use of products from the deadly nightshade or poppy. To stimulate the appetite, there are chicory, balm or thyme. Elder, boxwood, ivy and mercury plants are laxatives—as is the notorious product made from the seeds of the castor-oil plant. For the opposite effect, one might use the strawberry, white nettle, periwinkle, or campanula.

For aching eyes, there are eyewashes made of cornflowers, plantains or rose petals. Skin troubles, burns, cuts and abrasions can be treated by plants. Plants used to help a fever are known as febrifuges.

For tonics, there are artemisia, juniper, gentian, daisy, sage and many others which have elaborate names but are so common that people trample over them without a thought as they walk through the fields and woods.

The study of herbs involves every illness, every cure, and every item in the doctor's vocabulary. But obviously no one can use these medicines without knowing exactly how to prepare them: how long the flowers or leaves should remain in the water, whether the water should be boiling or not, and so on.

Acquiring this expertise takes time and patience. Most people think it is better to go to the pharmacist instead. But it is worth remembering that the same herbs from the fields and the woods are sometimes incorporated in his potions, pills and lotions.

These plants are among the best-known herbs. However, research by botanists and chemists shows that nearly all plants, by virtue of the rare substances they contain, can be of service in the war against disease. Very often, the elaborate names on the pharmacist's labels represent humble plants that attract little attention in fields or woods.

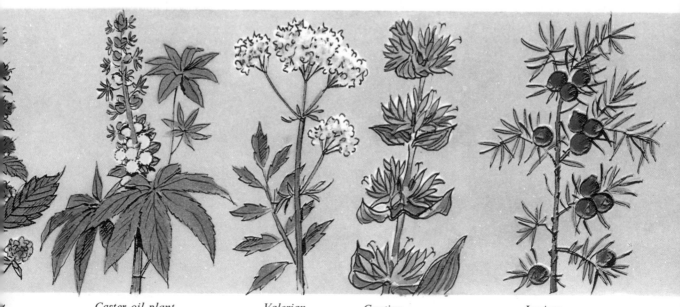

Caster-oil plant   Valerian   Gentian   Juniper

Nature's Surprises

In our trip through the months we have discussed plants and animals from most of the main groups, but some of nature's creations are so strange that they defy classification.

There is, for instance, a kind of insect called a tardigrade (which means slow-moving). It resembles a spider; it measures only one twenty-fifth of an inch across and yet it lives, moves, reproduces and has eight legs just like any other spider. But this particular spider has one very strange characteristic. When there is a prolonged dry spell, all trace of moisture disappears from its body. It dries out completely and blows about in the breeze like a speck of dust, apparently lifeless. No matter what you do to it, there is no reaction. But when rain falls again, this speck of dust absorbs water and swells and comes to life again, after weeks of

Some of nature's surprises: carnivorous plants. Above is the sundew and below is the Venus's flytrap in the process of catching and digesting an insect.

inactivity. It is sometimes hard to draw the dividing line between life and death.

Then there is the dipnoan, or lungfish, which lives in ponds and rivers. It lives like a fish, breathing by means of gills, but if the pond should dry up completely in the summer or if the river water should become a mere trickle, the dipnoan buries itself in the mud and can survive there in an air pocket even if the mud becomes baked as hard as concrete. The dipnoan switches over to breathing by air because it is equipped with both gills and lungs. It becomes a land animal as long as the drought lasts, but once the water flows again, it goes back to being a fish. It is difficult to decide whether to list the dipnoan with the fish or the amphibians. Most zoologists call it a fish but agree that it is more like an amphibian than any other fish.

The Australian duck-billed platypus is another strange creature. It has lungs, not gills

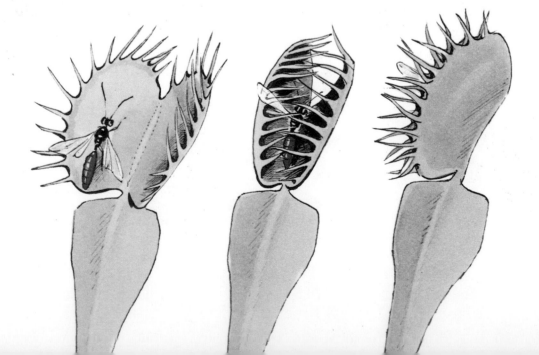

and lives amphibiously. It swims through the water with the aid of its four webbed feet, each equipped with fives toes. It is covered with fur and has mammary glands for suckling its young, so it must be a mammal. Yet it has a sort of snout which looks like a duck's bill and it lays eggs as birds and reptiles do. The duck-billed platypus seems to be both mammal and bird.

Nature's creatures are often surprising and sometimes even comical, but a group of plants exists which are quite astonishing. One of these is the sundew, which grows in marshy places. It has white flowers and round, reddish-colored leaves on the end of long stems. There are rows of hairs on the leaves, and each hair has what appears to be a drop of dew at its tip. In fact, this is a special sticky fluid produced by glands at the base of the hairs and its purpose is to trap insects that land on the leaf. As an insect struggles to free itself, it irritates the glands and the whole leaf closes up around it like jaws. The insect is digested by sap in the hollow

The duck-billed platypus (above) lives amphibiously but lays eggs and is actually a mammal. The dipnoan (below) seems to be a fish, but it has a pair of lungs in reserve and can live without water in an emergency.

center of the leaf and, when the leaf reopens, there is no trace of the insect. The Venus's fly-trap is another such carnivorous plant; it is found in North America. These are plants that, to some extent, feed as animals do.

There are luminous toadstools, luminous insects and luminous fish. There are insects that can live in the ice at very high altitudes and others that are at home in crude oil. There is even a fish equipped with a suction pad so that it can get a lift by attaching itself to another fish or even a boat. The ways of nature are ingenious and endlessly fascinating.

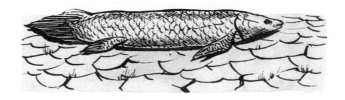

DECEMBER

The Antipodes

There is no top or bottom on a ball that never stops rolling and this is true of the Earth. For everyone on the Earth, "bottom" is the central point where all their vertical wells would eventually meet if they could all dig down deep enough. "Top" is what is above everybody's head. There is no question of people on the opposite side of the globe falling off or standing on their heads. Everyone is held firmly in position, feet downward, by a force which pulls all objects toward the center of the Earth. This force is called gravity.

But it is true that, in one sense, life in places on the other side of the equator (known as the antipodes, which means "having the feet opposite") is the opposite to ours, even though the people there do have their feet firmly anchored on the ground by gravity. While we have winter, they have summer. That is true, for instance, in Australia and New Zealand. On June 21st, when we are enjoying our longest day at the summer solstice, they are living through their winter solstice and their longest night. Christmas in the Northern Hemisphere is always associated with snow and cold, but Christmas comes at the hottest time of the year in the antipodes.

Each single day the people of the antipodes experience conditions opposite to ours; their day coincides with our night and their night with our day. The contrast between conditions in the two hemispheres is most marked at the poles, where six months of daylight contrast with six months of darkness. As you leave the poles and move in the direction of the equator, the differences are less marked: for instance, a region that is experiencing only two months of continuous daylight has an opposite region situated at the same distance from the other pole that is having two months of uninterrupted darkness. The eighteen-hour night experienced in one latitude in the Northern Hemisphere corresponds with an eighteen-hour day at the same latitude in the Southern Hemisphere. As you move nearer to the equator, the differences grow less until, once within the area bounded by the tropics, all places have twelve hours of darkness, twelve hours of daylight.

In spite of all the variations, every point on the globe has a total of exactly six months of daylight and six months of darkness in one year. It is surprising that things work out so fairly. Unfortunately, this does not happen when it is a question of temperature. Different parts of the globe receive very different treatment in this respect, but here again, there is a parallel between the Northern Hemisphere and the Southern Hemisphere. On the southern side of the equator at the same latitude as that of temperate North America, there is a similar temperate zone. The same crops can grow and the same animals thrive; and the same sort of houses are built to protect the inhabitants from the same sort of climate. Life there corresponds in many ways with life in temperate North America, though the seasons are still opposite, of course.

Thanks to air travel, it is now possible to escape in a matter of hours from winter fog and storms to a sunny summer beach in a warmer area. Today strawberries and cherries, oranges and bananas appear on the table in

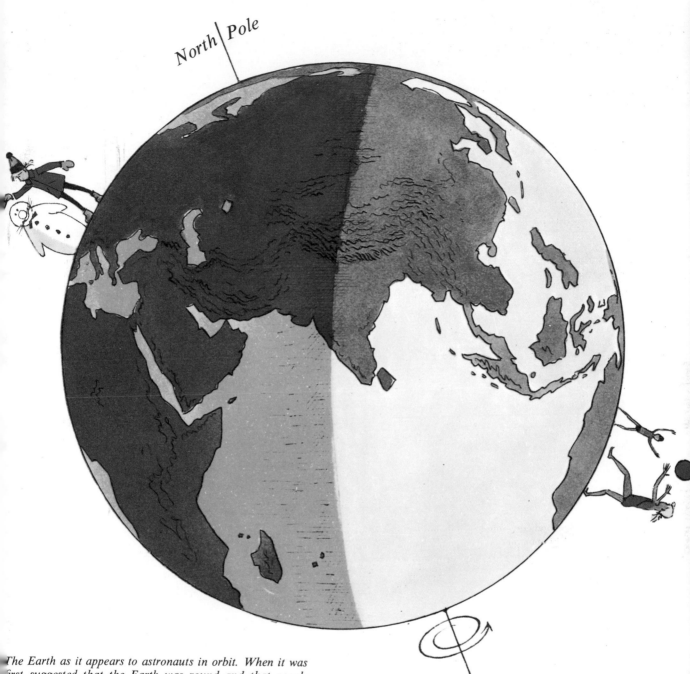

North Pole

The Earth as it appears to astronauts in orbit. When it was first suggested that the Earth was round and that people lived on the opposite side of it, no one could imagine how it was possible because those people would be living upside down. Now it is understood that, because of the pull of gravity, people all over the world live the right way up.

wintry lands where they could never grow naturally at that time and in seasons when no fresh fruit would normally be available. Even when one part of the globe is dormant, other parts are productive. Man and nature are working together increasingly to see that the entire population of the world can benefit from everything that the world can produce.

DECEMBER

Camouflage

Many animals have external features which are so well matched to their surroundings that the animals are practically invisible; others can change color with the seasons to fit in with the changes in their surroundings, and a few are equipped with some mysterious device which causes them to change their color from minute to minute to minute, as they pass over different colored backgrounds.

The best-known of this last group is the chameleon, a kind of lizard which lives in warm regions. It is fascinating to watch this little animal change color. It can change from yellowish-white, by way of green and brown, to almost black. In its natural surroundings, the chameleon turns yellow as it crosses the sand and green as it climbs onto a bush. This is a very clever and effective defense mechanism.

The stoat is a representative of the group of animals whose coats change with the seasons. In summer its fur is a sandy-brown color, but as winter approaches in snowy northern climates it turns white.

There are many creatures, in all groups of the animal kingdom, whose coloring is permanently matched to their surroundings. Butterflies are sometimes splashed with the bright colors of the flowers on which they alight, while their nocturnal cousins, the moths, are the somber

Top left is the chameleon, which changes color according to its background. Below it is the stoat, shown in winter and summer coloring. The stick insect at the foot of the page is permanently disguised as a twig.

146

The leopard merges into the background of changing light and shade provided by the leaves.

gray-and-brown shades of twilight and of the bark on which they sit. The larvae and chrysalises are the colors of their usual hiding places, so that they appear to be just another pebble on the ground, another bud on a tree or another piece of gray lichen on an old stump.

The zebra that roams the plains of Africa has black and cream stripes on its body resembling the shadows that are cast by the tall grasses of its habitat.

The leopard prowls through wooded country; its spotted coat resembles shadows thrown by the leaves in the mingled light and shade beneath the trees.

When you look down at the seabed, there seems to be nothing but sand, slightly rippled by the movement of the water, yet a fisherman's net may uncover the flattened fawny-gray body of a ray. Shellfish live against a very different background; their shells have the color

and rough texture of the rocks to which they cling.

Perhaps the most cleverly disguised of all creatures are the stick insects. It is possible to stare right at one without realizing that it is there. Even when a slight movement betrays it, you can lose sight of it almost at once. These insects are long and slender, with very fine long legs and wings. Poised on a twig, they look just like part of the tree.

These natural devices by which creatures are matched to the colors of their surroundings are known as mimicry. There are many other tricks used in self-defense; many animals, for instance, try to make themselves look fierce and alarming when they are threatened. When the cat senses danger, its back arches and its fur stands out all over its body—an instinctive trick which makes it appear much larger than it really is in an attempt to frighten the enemy.

147

Christmas Plants— and Lichens

The gardens look bare. Dahlias and chrysanthemums which flowered late into the fall have now withered and the tubers and roots have been brought in out of the cold. There is not a single splash of vivid color left. The sameness of the browns and blacks of the soil and branches is only broken by the odd bush which is still green because its leaves are so strong and hardy that they can withstand the frost. At this bleak time of the year the dark green, glossy leaves of such trees as the boxwood, laurel and holly are particularly appreciated. The coniferous trees—yews, larches, pines and firs—also keep their leaves right through the winter. In a few days preparations for Christmas will begin and the fir and holly will have places of honor in the house.

There is one form of vegetation, the lichen, that is unaffected by the changing seasons, but it is rather drab and does not add much color to the winter scene. It has neither stem, nor leaves, nor flowers. It can be seen growing in woods, on tree trunks and low branches. It can even survive on rocks far into the polar regions and high up in the mountains above the snowline. It is the only form of vegetation that can withstand such unfriendly conditions.

Lichens assume various forms. They may branch out from one anchor point on a log or a rock, or they may form clumps which are loosely attached to the base at several points, or they may spread over the base like a hard crust. They may be yellow, brown, black or greenish in color; in fact, lichens look more like rust or mold than plants. Because they look so simple, one would expect them to be very primitive organisms, the protozoa of the plant world, but this is not the case.

A lichen is not a simple single unit; it is a team of two, and the two members of the team

Dog lichen

Cup lichen

Two Christmas plants: holly (facing page) and mistletoe (right). Food is scarce in December, and the thrush is lucky to find these white mistletoe berries.

are dependent on each other. One member is an alga, belonging to the same group of plants as the algae of the sea. Because the alga contains chlorophyll, it can process carbon dioxide drawn from the air, so its role is to produce the food that is necessary for the team. The second member of the team is a fungus. Since it contains no chlorophyll and grows on deadwood or rock, it has no source of food, so it depends on the alga to provide food. In exchange, the fungus spreads over the alga, shielding it from attack and keeping it moist so that it does not dry up and die.

It is because lichens are really two plants that they come in so many different forms. The shape and color of each lichen are determined by which particular alga associates with which fungus.

It is also because lichens consist of two organisms working together that they can survive in such difficult conditions. They can withstand cold, drought or any other extremes in climate, which is why they are the last plants to succumb to hostile conditions and the first to establish themselves again.

There are other plants that cannot survive unaided, but they manage to keep alive by being ruthless. Unlike the two members of the lichen team, they live off another organism without contributing anything in return. These plants are called parasites. They have no proper roots and they live by attaching themselves to another plant and feeding on its sap. Mistletoe is a parasite. It often grows on apple trees. Together with the holly, mistletoe is given a special place at Christmastime.

These are not artistic designs, or plant flowers, or patterns for lacemaking. They are snow crystals that were produced by the action of cold upon water vapor. These crystals *unite to form snowflakes. However elaborate the finished patterns turn out to be, snow crystals always conform to the rule and have six points.*

DECEMBER

Winter "Flowers": Snowflakes

There is one type of "flower" that makes an appearance only at the coldest time of the year. It is as beautiful as the other flowers but you need to examine it closely to be able to see its beauty; a magnifying glass is a great help. It is a flower from the sky, not from the earth. Its name is snow, and calling it a flower is really not too far-fetched.

One day the earth and sky are gray and dull. The next, as if by magic, everything is transformed. Snow has fallen during the night and turned yesterday's drab scene into a beautiful, shining white landscape. Like flower petals, the snowflakes whirl around as they float down from the sky. When they settle on the ground, they form a thick carpet that deadens all sounds.

The falling snowflakes look as light as thistledown but their appearance is deceptive. They are made of frozen water vapor and they will become water again when the thaw comes. Water is heavy—one cubic foot of it weighs over sixty-two pounds. So it is wise to keep a check on any surfaces that have to support this thick white blanket.

In the mountains the weight of collected snow can have terrifying results. A mass of snow can suddenly fall away from a peak and crash down the mountainside, carrying loose rock along with it. This roaring, hurtling mass is an avalanche which can destroy everything in its path, burying animals and people, houses and roads.

Snow is not always destructive or purely decorative. It serves a very useful purpose when it settles on fields and gardens. It is like covering the soil with a cellular blanket to keep it warm. Snow crystals contain a lot of air, just as a blanket does, and the still air trapped inside prevents frosty air penetrating through the snow to the ground. It therefore protects shoots and seeds from frost. Snow is so effective at keeping out the cold that Eskimos use it to build their igloos and mountaineers rub their fingers and ears with it when they are threatened with frostbite.

Snow can be fun. It brings new opportunities for games and sports: snowballing, building snowmen, sledding and skiing. But anyone who pauses for a moment to look at the substance

hat makes all these things possible may be astonished by what he sees. A snowflake is a cluster of snow crystals, and every crystal is a work of art—and, what is more, it is unique. It is like a piece of fine lace or embroidery or exquisite filigree work. Yet even though no two crystals are exactly alike, they all have one thing in common: all have six points branching out from a central point: they are hexagonal.

A snow crystal forms when cold causes water vapor in clouds to freeze, usually around a central point (such as a speck of dust). The variety of patterns is infinite but the basic hexagonal form of each crystal is predetermined, just as the design of a flower is. A pear seed must produce a flower typical of the Papilionaceae family; from a dandelion seed grows a flower of the Compositae group; a carrot seed without fail produces a flower of the Umbelliferae type; a water "seed" produces a six-pointed snowflake. All natural substances that form crystals do so according to a rule, no matter whether they are sugar, salt, soda, sulphur or snow. Snow is clearly not a living thing, but in view of the special nature of its growth, it does not seem too fanciful to compare it to a flower.

151

DECEMBER

Winter Solstice

The North Pole is in darkness. Gradually, since the autumn equinox, the area of land that has no light all day long has grown larger until, in late December, people living in some towns in northern Europe have to live and work in total darkness. A few hours' northward flight by jet—and one plunges into a black abyss!

In the United States and most of Canada, there is never a day without daylight, but in midwinter daylight may last for nine hours or less. The sun rises and sets at more or less the same point on the horizon, making only a small arc in the sky and shedding little warmth or light. The pale sunshine hardly affects the grip of the ice and frost.

If the movement of the Earth were to continue along the same lines for just a few weeks longer, more of the Northern Hemisphere would be plunged into continuous darkness.

Even though people who live in very northern latitudes have to spend much of their winters in darkness, they are often treated to one of nature's most spectacular shows—the aurora borealis, or the northern lights.

People living in the temperate regions of the Northern Hemisphere don't often get to see these shifting, flame-like curtains of red or green lights which make the dark winter night almost as bright as day. Their winter nights can often be very drab and gray.

Fortunately, however, December brings the winter solstice, which marks the longest night and the shortest day, and from now on the Northern Hemisphere starts to move nearer to the sun again. People in this part of the world can now look forward to spring, and the festi

Everything looks dead: the earth sleeps under its blanket of snow; the sun rises low over the horizon, pale and with little warmth; the robin comes to our window begging for a few crumbs, the titmouse for morsels of fat. But despite the drab scene and seemingly bleak outlook, it is a time of promise.

...val of Christmas seems an especially well-timed opportunity for celebrating.

Christmas is the celebration of a birth and, by a happy coincidence, it also marks the new beginning of life in the Northern Hemisphere. The nights are long, but the streets and houses are full of light.

Hanukkah, the Jewish Festival of Lights, is also celebrated at this time of year. Each day at sundown a candle called the *shamash* is used to light another candle. The celebration lasts eight days. By the end of the festival, nine bright candles stand together in the dark winter night.

The New Year comes as another reminder that, although much of the landscape looks drab and desolate, nature on our hemisphere will soon reawaken. Just as the days, the seasons and the years continue their endless cycles and are continually renewed, so life on Earth begins and progresses all over again. Plants, animals, fishes, birds, insects and man all take part in the fascinating changes that happen in every month of the year.

After December another year begins, with its seasons, its flowers and its fruits. Christmas and the New Year are times for celebration; they promise new life.

153

Index

155